Alice Mary Lovat

Clare Vaughan

Alice Mary Lovat
Clare Vaughan
ISBN/EAN: 9783744653206
Printed in Europe, USA, Canada, Australia, Japan
Cover: Foto ©ninafisch / pixelio.de

More available books at **www.hansebooks.com**

BY
LADY LOVAT

A NEW EDITION WITH ORIGINAL ILLUSTRATIONS AND
SOME HITHERTO UNPUBLISHED LETTERS

NEW YORK
THE CATHEDRAL LIBRARY ASSOCIATION
1896.

Copyright, Joseph H. McMahon, 1896.

PREFACE.

When the writer of this beautiful life asked of me to add a few words by way of preface, I could not refuse; but I little knew what I was promising. Nothing can be added which will not take away something of the completeness and beauty of the book.

The life of Sister Mary Clare is truly Franciscan in the love of poverty and the love of God. It reads like another chapter in the "Little Flowers of St. Francis," breathing the same charity, joy, and peace in the Holy Ghost.

Neither sorrow nor suffering, though of both Mary Clare had much, ever darkened her joy. It came from the unchanging love of her Divine Master and her longing soon to see Him in the eternal rest.

This book is a witness to the world of the sanctity of the only Church of Jesus Christ, for on no other stem do such fruits grow. It is a sample of the homes of Catholic England, imperishable through centuries of penal laws and the proud contempt of the world that knew them not. It is also a standard by which to measure the true Christian life, and the high aspiration of Catholic faith. And in this it is both a rebuke to many

PREFACE.

homes and hearts at this day, and a voice full of encouragement and of strength, saying to us all, "Come up hither." What St. Agnes was to the men and women of Rome, Mary Clare may be to us in these relaxing days in England.

HENRY EDWARD,
Cardinal Archbishop.

WESTMINSTER, *Aug. 7th,* 1887.

PREFACE TO THE AMERICAN EDITION.

There are sufficient reasons for publishing this new edition of Clare Vaughan's beautiful life by Lady Lovat. In the first place, it is not as widely known as it deserves, especially among those to whom it might become an incentive to search after that precious pearl of the religious life, which grows daily more rare amid the numerous devices of modern worldliness, ever eager to discredit the spirit of Christian self-sacrifice. We have come to view the systematic cultivation of bodily comforts and of physical enjoyment as both a necessity and a duty which must not be interfered with by the obligations of religion; and that, whatever allowance we may make for the spiritual aspirations and devout practices of past generations, this enlightened age has outgrown the need and, indeed, the capacity of bodily mortification and self-imposed humiliation. Clare Vaughan stands in evidence against this spirit of our age; and if there be in her actions, at times, that which must seem to us extravagant, let us remember that love is impulsive, and that the more intense it is, the less can we make it accountable to the exactions of mere human prudence. No one assumes that the extraordinary outbursts of divine passion in heroic souls are written down in order to cause the reader to imitate them. They are intended only as proofs of the quality of a love which forgets self in its longing for union with God, a longing which we all are placed on earth to kindle in our hearts by prayer and fidelity to grace.

The present volume has been enriched by some hitherto unpublished letters from Clare Vaughan to Miss Bellasis, a nun of the Holy Child Jesus, and by a few extracts from other sources.

For the illustrations, we are indebted to the kindness of Father Kenelm Vaughan, and to the courtesy of the Superioress of the Convent of Poor Clares at Amiens, where the beautiful blossom of Clare's vocation unfolded under the influence of the Perpetual Adoration of the Most Blessed Sacrament. There, at the foot of the altar, she placed the scarcely opened flower of her innocent life, and the sweet fragrance of her truly heroic virtues still pervades the secluded spot. May its perfumes be carried across the ocean to the young and pure in heart of our land, to the lovers of the Blessed Sacrament, and to all those who long for the "Kingdom come," which is opened only to the humble of heart and the mortified!

INTRODUCTION.

To some of us God has given, once in our lives, to know one of His hidden saints, and though, perhaps—life is so busy, we cannot always stop to learn the lessons it brings us—we have passed on unconscious or only half-conscious of the meaning of the gift, yet the time comes when we pause and find out what He has given us, and then perchance taken away.

It is of one of these chosen souls, hidden, indeed, except to a privileged few, that the following sketch is written. To the little circle in which she lived, Clare Vaughan was in truth the bright moving example as she is now its most beloved memory. Many have done greater things for God in the world's sight, have striven and fought and conquered in harder fields of battle, and have found a far wider field for their activities. Hers was very small; she was hardly known outside the immediate circle of her friends and relations, and latterly to the Community of Poor Clares at Amiens. Of the outside world she knew nothing. For her it contained only one Object of interest, one Model for imitation—Jesus Christ. What He loved and came to save she also loved—sinners; and because He had "nothing to do with the world," without knowing it she hated it, and in this is contained the lesson of her life. Simple and unpretending as it was in other respects, it preached with a voice which never faltered the great truth which none can learn too quickly or too well, that there is in God's creation but one Object of love, which is Himself. He only is worthy of our hearts who made them; below, and at the root of everything else, there is ever "*le vide et le néant,*" and no one could come in contact with Clare without learning something of this. She *constrained* people to love God better, she made them love the things she loved—such as mortification, self-denial, etc.—because she herself saw in these things only the means (which gave them an irresistible charm in her eyes) of making herself like to Him who took on Him all our sins, and "by whose stripes we are healed."

She did not reason about her love; it belonged to her as part of her being to love beautiful things—nature, music, and above all, poetry; and as these things did not satisfy her panting soul, most of all she loved Him; and as He wept with Martha and Mary, and rejoiced at Cana and feasted with Zaccheus, so she also threw herself heart and soul into the sorrows and joys and trials of those with whom she lived, and was "all things to all men" that she might win souls to God. This feature in her character shows itself most prominently in her letters, and forms their charm. There is no aiming at effect, above all, no attempt at preaching; only the tenderest interest in all the concerns of the persons to whom she is writing, and the most heartfelt sympathy in their troubles and joys. Still, through

INTRODUCTION. ix

all this, and mingling with it, we can always detect the presence of what may be called the master passion, the "note" of her life: "Let us love the Lord Our God with our whole heart, and our whole soul, and with all our mind"; and then when the truth, so long hoped-for, so eagerly expected, dawned upon her: "For a night cometh when no man may work."

"Precious in the sight of God," we are told by the Scriptures, "is the death of His saints"; and if the prophet speaks so of the death of the saints, are we to suppose that their lives are less beautiful and pleasing to Him, or less full of edification to us?

The Mohammedans, it is said, pick up carefully every piece of paper they come across, lest the name of God should be written on it and trampled under foot. Should we do less with the lives of the elect, on whom the name of God is written, not once, but many times? Should we not rather treasure them up, keeping them before our eyes, trying to learn the lesson they may have for *us*? It may be urged Clare Vaughan is not a canonized saint, and it is far from our intention to claim any such title for her; still, is there not room for all in God's Church? And while the many seek instructions from the lives of the St. Teresas and St. Francis de Sales, the St. Catherines and St. Augustines, may not the few possibly find in these annals of one who was, as it were, one of themselves, only a purer, higher, better self, a comfort and encouragement in times of difficulty such as their spiritual needs require?

Perhaps, too, this little sketch may succeed in reviving in some hearts who knew her that influence, ever for good, which she exerted whilst on earth. And if, also, the smallest increase of the love of God be awakened in the heart of one of Christ's little ones whilst reading it, it will not have been written in vain; and for those who loved her it will be a comfort to think that her work on earth is not ended, and that " being dead, she speaketh."

CLARE VAUGHAN.

CHAPTER I.

CLARE VAUGHAN was born in the year 1843. The first years of her life were spent at her father's residence on the banks of the River Wye. Her first recollections, therefore, were of scenes of great natural beauty : the river which ran at the foot of the hill, at ten minutes' distance from the house ; the meadows, where one waded ankle deep, in the spring, through cowslips ; the great elms and limes—

"A summer home of murmurous wings,"

and added to this all the charm of innocent country amusements, such as make a different being of a country child from a town one. The frantic delight in the daily games of hide-and-seek among the bushes, when the lessons were over, the bird-nesting, the happy scrambling existence altogether, which made life a perpetual feast, and which asked nothing of the outer world but that it should leave it to itself. Such was Clare's life, from the time she could remember anything to the time she was ten years old. Her golden age, and long afterwards, when nothing remained but a "memory and a hope," her greatest happiness was to talk of those wonderful days of magic happiness (for so it seemed to her in comparison with the trials that succeeded it), and of the sainted mother who used to talk to them so beautifully and so enthusiastically of God and His service, and of the unutterable happiness of leaving all to follow Him. Of this dear mother, Clare was never tired of talking. She was the central figure of that happy group, and more than all the world to each one of them.

Nothing that could be said of Clare would have any completeness unless it spoke also of her mother. Her mother's beautiful soul reflected itself on Clare's as in a faithful mirror. All Clare's likes and dislikes, which were enthusiastic, vehement—as it was in her nature to be about everything,—were learnt at her mother's knee; and time, which strengthens strong things, though it effaces weak ones, took nothing from this holy and powerful influence—rather adding to it,—so that to the end it remained the paramount one of her life.

To the blessing of a holy mother Clare joined that of an excellent Christian father. It is not too much to say of both, that their one object in life was to bring up their children in the love and fear of God. Worldly ideas and maxims were far from their lips, and the secluded life they led enabled them to give up a great part of their time to their children. As to Mrs. Vaughan, she never ceased from putting before them the joys and attractions of a holy life, and especially of religious vocation. As her children grew up, at the time when parents are generally occupied in plans for their advancement in life, hers were only directed to their getting a higher place in the kingdom of Heaven.

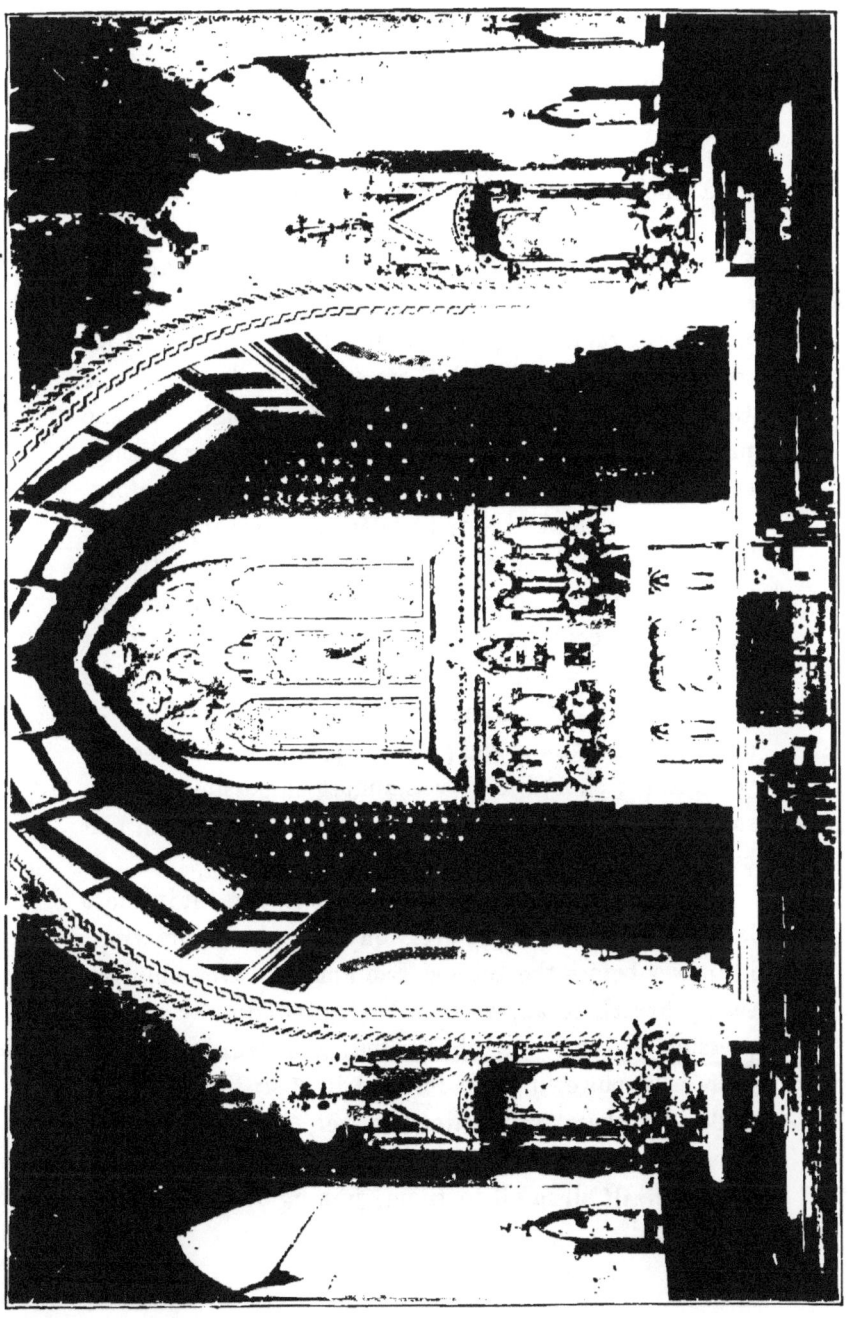

Far from having that natural desire of most parents, of seeing their children marry and settle in life in order to perpetuate their name (in this case an old and honored one), *her* only wish was that all her children— sons and daughters—should become priests and nuns. She used to say that she did not wish to give less than all to Him who had given all to her. She never wearied of reminding them that gifts and talents of all sorts were only given to them to be made use of for God, and used often to recall their thoughts to the presence of God, and to the duty of sanctifying all their actions by offering them to His greater honor and glory.

Mrs. Vaughan had a great talent for drawing, and in her younger days used to delight her friends with her portraits and caricatures. As she advanced in holiness her tender conscience dreaded a possible breach of charity to her neighbor. She felt it was impossible to exercise it without sometimes hurting the feelings of others; so gradually she gave it up, and in the last few years of her short life it was almost impossible to persuade her to indulge a taste which in her youth had been almost a passion.

Her growth in mortification and detachment in those latter days was marked; every day she spent hours wrapt in prayer before the Blessed Sacrament. Her children seeing her there absorbed in God, carried away an impression never to be obliterated, and which in after years bore powerful fruit for God in their lives.

Besides these recollections of her, her children had others, beautiful and ineffaceable. She knew how to make herself all in all to them, joining in their games and amusements, reading poetry with them, and singing to them.

How willingly we would linger upon those bright days, the brightest of Clare's life, the little taste of happiness without which no one's life seems, or perhaps is, complete! The end, however, was near. Who is it that has said that upon all earthly things are written the words, "passing away"? And so it was with that happy, united circle. We have already spoken of her—the mother—and of what she was to her children; of her hidden life with God we cannot speak, but those who knew her best recognized, talking of those days, that she was, in the truest sense of the word, ripe for Heaven. Indeed, an intimate friend, who had the opportunity of being thoroughly acquainted with her spiritual life, said afterwards that he had seen her so visibly increasing in sanctity and detatchment during the last few months of her life, that he almost wondered that no dim fear or suspicion had come over him of what was at hand. Her children, however, naturally knew nothing of this, and the blow, when it came, found them totally unprepared.

It was in the winter of the year 1853. One day they were told that they had another brother. Later on they flocked in—as they had always done—to their mother's room, as happy and noisy as usual. Mrs. Vaughan, after talking and listening to them for a while, had complained of fatigue. They were sent away, and at first she tried with a faithful friend, who was watching by her, to say Vespers and Compline. Had she come to the *Nunc Dimittis*, touching finale after the day's efforts, and in *her* case so strikingly appropriate? We are not told; but we know that after a time ever-increasing pain warned those who were with her that danger was to be apprehended, and after a very short period of suspense they knew that all hope had vanished. A few short hours more and, praying fervently to the last, her beautiful soul went home. For her, indeed, there was an Eternal Home, but for some at least whom she left behind, earth could never more be anything but a place of exile. Their home was with her. Thank God! we can think of them now as re-united in the blissful enjoyment of the Beatific Vision for evermore.

We hardly dare to picture to ourselves the scene which followed in that desolate house. The father, almost beside himself with agony, going into the schoolroom where his children were assembled praying, and telling them they had no mother. Thus suddenly were they called upon to practise heroic virtue, which till then they only knew in name.

Jean Paul Richter says that " with our first act of self-renunciation life begins." We may accordingly date a new epoch in Clare's life from this moment. Till then all life had smiled upon her; she was now to learn something of its frowns. Not that she had no troubles till that time, for what child of a sensitive temperament (which hers was essentially by nature) has not had something to bear long before she is ten years of age, and what sorrows are harder to bear *for the moment* than children's? But till then she had always been sure of sympathy; she had always her mother to go to. Now she had to learn to stand alone. We shall see by what means she contrived to do so. Very soon after this overwhelming loss, another, small indeed by comparison with the first, and yet of great consequence to all her after-life, occurred. They were no longer to live at Courtfield. Their home, with all its beautiful memories, was to become itself a memory; and though they were thus spared the pang of seeing the same round of duties coming and returning, the same rooms and spots occupied by the same people though emptied of that beloved presence for evermore, yet this entire severance from the place they cared most for in the world was not without its anguish as well. It had, however, one salutary effect: it prevented all that morbid clinging to the outward garments and show of sorrow which so often remains long after the soul, as it were, is gone. And of this feeling, which has no religion in it, Clare was always singularly devoid. She never nursed her grief; it was present with her to the last day of her life, as a loss which she never could get over, as love which she never could replace; but this was not from habit, but because her mother really was everything to her, humanly speaking, and she kept this place in her affections to the last. And the impression, instead of getting fainter as her life declined, on the contrary—as she was once heard to say, appeared to strengthen as the time of their reunion drew near; as we may have noticed that features of an absent face, when we know we are going to see it again very soon, seem all at once to brighten in our recollection of them, as if the approaching form had rubbed from our memories something of the dust which time had collected on it. It

was the one earthly tie she clung to, to the last; and it is on this account that we dwell upon it at such length in this early chapter of her life, because it was in sober truth the key-note to her life, the *raison d'être* of a great deal which otherwise might appear exaggerated and unreal.

The day of their departure from Courtfield was settled. They took their last look at the chapel where they had first prayed by their mother's side; of the room where they had seen her for the last time; of all the beloved spots endeared to them by a thousand recollections; and with intelligences sharpened beyond their years by the sudden agony of sorrow, "the valley of the shadow of death," through which they had so lately passed, they took their last look at Courtfield. For Clare it was the last she was ever to take of her home. She never saw Courtfield again. The uprooting was accomplished. She was nevermore to have a home except where the Blessed Sacrament was. There, was to be henceforward her only resting-place. He, who said that He would not always leave us orphans, now possessed her whole heart. She had already, on making her First Communion, inspired by the grace of God and her mother's prayers, offered herself to be His spouse if He would have her, and now He came to her, bearing the Cross, and she was to feel what it was that He, whom she called Lord and Master, expected from her.

The first place Clare and her brothers and sisters settled at, after leaving Courtfield, was Boulogne, where they remained nearly three years,—three dreary years taken up by the monotonous round of schoolroom duties, and diversified only by the daily constitutional on the ramparts, or an occasional excursion into the neighboring country. Clare never talked of this period of her life without a shudder. There was nothing for her to look forward to, nothing for her to hope for. She was very fond of reading; but they had taken very few books abroad with them, and it was difficult to procure others by English writers in a foreign country, so that she could not even have resource to that almost sovereign remedy against grief and ennui. . For French books, especially French story-books, composed expressly for the class *ingénue*, she had not much appreciation, and though she had some favorite authors in the religious world, and later on was to have unbounded admiration for the works of some of the great French ascetic writers, her tastes at that time were not sufficiently developed to allow her to appreciate these, or to find in them that stimulus which would have helped to lift her out of the dull, featureless existence which she now led.

One source of excitement the Vaughan family had, however, and Clare with them, in common with the whole of Europe. It was the time of the Crimean war, and outside their quiet household all was wildest excitement, continual reports contradicted as soon as spread, panics and rejoicings,—in fine, all the gay pageant on the one hand, and killing anxiety on the other, which makes war paramount, for the moment, over every other topic of interest. The reason of their sharing so deeply in the common interest lay in their father. He had gone to the seat of war, and though not joining in the actual conflict, was yet exposed to considerable personal danger; and in his letters, and the newspapers in which they read of the scenes which were actually passing before his eyes, lay the whole outer interest of their lives.

After they had been living more than two years and a half at Boulogne an event occurred which served, for a time at least, to break the routine of Clare's most monotonous life, and became a fruitful topic of conversation for some time afterwards.

The Weld Blundells, a family nearly related to them by ties of blood, and from that time still more nearly by those of friendship, were passing through Boulogne.

Clare and one of her sisters had not long recovered from scarlet fever; her cousins not having had it, a strict quarantine was kept, as far as actual contact was concerned, though they were allowed to meet and talk as much as they liked in the open air. The acquaintance then formed between Clare and one of her cousins ripened into a friendship which lasted for both their lives, and gave rise to a correspondence of which ample use will be made later.

In the following spring, 1856, Clare and her brothers and sisters returned to England, and Courtfield being shut up—Colonel Vaughan finding it impossible to make up his mind to return to the scenes of his past happiness,—a house was taken for them in London, in the neighborhood of the Oratory, and later, one in Montague Square, and there they remained for some years. Great was the joy of the Vaughan family at returning to their own country. There, at least, they were sure of seeing their two elder brothers, one of whom was a secular priest, and the other a Benedictine monk;* and to Clare, in addition to the general cause of rejoicing, there was the special one that she was now within reach of her beloved books, her father having, whilst dismantling Courtfield, taken most of his library to London. With her books and the occasional visits of friends, some of whom dated from the happy days now for ever gone, Clare was, comparatively speaking, happy. What was more to her, though, than books or friends, was the neighborhood of the Oratory. There, absorbed in adoration before the Blessed Sacrament, she used to go and spend all the time allowed to her by her governess, and which could be spared from her studies and the other duties of her life. In the first letter we have of hers, which is addressed to the friend N——, of whom we have already spoken, she alludes to it. It is dated July, 1857. After answering some question which has been addressed to her by her correspondents, she continues:

"But, dear N——, the Blessed Sacrament will teach you everything. Do not forget me when you go before His Most Holy Presence. Try to let nothing content you but God alone. You were created but to love Him —give Him then your whole heart. He is so beautiful, so worthy of our wretched love, and yet He asks for our love, for our hearts—and how many refuse Him? Pray to the Blessed Virgin to help you; you know what a loving Mother she is. Pray to her to teach you how to suffer little crosses and annoyances for the love of her

* The first is the Bishop of Salford, the second the late Archbishop of Sydney, N. S. W.

dying Son; how to meditate on His sufferings, as she did under the cross; and how to despise all but God and what is for His glory."

She adds, a little later on:

" I don't half like sending you this letter, for I am afraid you will think it too much of a sermon."

In the course of this year, 1857, another sacrifice was asked of Clare—her eldest sister, Gladys, went to be a nun. Gladys was one of those holy souls who had grown up in the shadow of her retired home as in the " closed garden " of which the Spouse of the Canticle speaks. Known only to a very few, she was to them as "the sweet odor of Christ," attracting souls to the service of her divine Master. Cardinal Wiseman, speaking of her to a friend, said he was always put in mind by her beauty and innocence, when he saw her, of what Eve must have been before the fall. She also, like Clare, had made up her mind, since her earliest years, to consecrate herself to God, and only waited till she should be old enough for the permission to be accorded to her of leaving all to follow Christ. Whilst living at Boulogne she had made acquaintance with the Community of Visitation Nuns at Marquetra. The sweet and loving spirit of St. Francis of Sales, which is so perfectly carried out and exemplified by the daughters of St. Jane Frances Chantal, seemed exactly intended to meet the wants of this holy soul. She was professed in the year 1859, and died a most edifying death in the same convent in the year 1879. The following lines were composed by her brother Roger when she went to be a nun:

The child heard a voice of love
Come from the throne above—
"Child, give thy heart and thy soul unto Me;
Leave thy own fatherland,
Leave that young happy band,
So loved and so cherished from childhood by thee.

"Friends that have loved thee, leave,
Hearts that will throb and grieve,
Souls that have thought thee their happiness here;
Leave, child, the well-known face,
Break from the friend's embrace,
Leave all on earth that thou holdest most dear.

"For I will thy portion be,
Yes! I will be loved by thee—
I, who have bought thee by suffering, from hell;
Earth alone shalt thou fear,
I alone will be dear,—
Turn to Me, child, who have loved thee so well."

To the voice that it wondering heard
The child answered not a word,
But near to its heart was this voice evermore.
Each day as it hurried by,
The same voice appeared to cry
Louder, more plaintive, more sweet than before.

And at length the child left its home,
And it went o'er the ocean foam,
To leave all it prized in the land of its birth,
To join in its Saviour's love,
To mingle with those above,
Who come to adore their Creator on earth.

CHAPTER II.

IT might be said of Clare that she had a special genius for friendship. The power of attracting and influencing others was part of her character, and showed itself from her earliest years; and as influence must be used for good or for evil, one is inclined to inquire what use she made of this talent,—whether she buried it in the ground, or, like the good servant, traded with it for her Master's benefit. Holy friendships seem to bear a special mark of God's approval, and to have, as it were, the mark of His divine blessing on them. We need not ransack our memories to call to mind the holy friendships of David and Jonathan, of St. Jerome and St. Paula, of St. Francis of Sales and St. Jane Chantal. These and a thousand others occur to us.

But for friendships to be blessed, they must be made in God and for God; and it was thus with Clare's. In her letters this is most strikingly exemplified. It never seems to occur to her that any other subject can be of equal interest or of any interest at all. Probably if any one had asked her the reason of her doing so, she would have answered, in' her earnest, enthusiastic way, "But what on earth else is there to write about?" Indeed, these things occupied all her heart, and seemingly left no room for any others. If it was so in her correspondence, this was equally observable in her conversation. When conversation (with her intimate friends) turned on religious topics, her interest kindled, her face glowed, all her mind and heart were in her words—in fact, her words could hardly come fast enough to give vent to all the thoughts that seemed to long to find utterance. This was especially the case when she talked of the love of Our Lord in remaining for ever with us in the Blessed Sacrament, and of His love for sinners. She was very fond of reading aloud, and was never so happy as when she had got one dear friend into a snug corner, and could then begin one of her favorite books, such as Dalgairns' "Book of the Sacred Heart," or Faber's "Foot of the Cross," or the "Following of Christ," or perhaps some favorite book of poetry. After a time the book used to be dropped, and she would begin, in her fervent way, talking of the beauty of Heaven, the goodness of God, and the joy of giving everything up for His sake. The only thing that ever restrained her, or made her suddenly stop short, was the fear that she might be thought to be preaching too much; then she used to break off in an agony, half humility and half fun. The great Rosmini's words might have been present with her: "Talk much with——; do not spare words, for words are the great means employed by Our Lord for instructing and animating men to good. In speaking of good things to others you will do good to your own soul, and become yourself more fervent in spirit. I take this thought from St. Augustine, who, in some part of his writings, says the same of himself."

Among the friends of Clare's father, for whom she had a special admiration, was Digby, the well-known writer of the *Mores Catholici*. She looked upon him as a sort of type of the Christian writer, a kind of chevalier *sans peur et sans reproche* of literature, and used to wade with the utmost perseverance through his solemn tomes. Another great writer, Dr. Ward, as well as his wife and daughter, were among her special friends, and some of the very few happy months—happy because they were spent in exquisite scenes of nature which she loved—were passed at their place in the Isle of Wight.

It was on one of these visits that an adventure happened of so striking a nature that it must not be omitted from this sketch of her life. On one occasion she and her friend were taking a long ramble together by the edge of the sea. Enrapt in their conversation, and not paying particular attention to where they were going, they suddenly discovered that they had wandered on to an extremely dangerous quicksand, and before they had time to retrace their steps they were up to their waists in it. To cry for help was vain—not a soul could be seen on the solitary beach; there was no help in sight, either by land or sea. In this agonizing extremity, a ghastly death almost within sight, Clare, seizing hold of a medal and scapular she wore, implored with the greatest fervor the help of Our Blessed Lady. Without being able to explain how it happened, she at once felt her feet on *terra firma*, and was able to rush off for assistance to the nearest cottage. So deeply was her friend imbedded in the treacherous mud that it was with great difficulty and some personal risk that her life was saved. Clare's acquaintance with Dr. Ward was of great use to her in many ways. He took the greatest interest in her theological studies, used to explain difficult passages to her, and recommend her what books to read. He also, in the course of one long visit which she paid in the spring of the year 1859, gave her lessons in Latin, which were of the greatest use to her afterwards.

In the following summer there was a plan mooted of her going to Ince Blundell, to spend a month with her uncle. She alludes to this in a letter she writes to N——. Apparently for the moment it was in abeyance.

"I thank you for your letter this morning. I *never* expected to go to Ince; in my heart I never thought I should go.... I want most awfully to read 'Lara' to you. It is so beautifully written; such an intensity of feeling and passion in it, and consequently *so melancholy*. I did not know I might read it till a few days ago. The worst of such books is that there is danger of their becoming *too* engrossing. I wonder if you will be surprised to hear that I am very fond of St. Philip. The great reason, I think, is that I have an intense devotion to the third Person of the Blessed Trinity, the Holy Ghost. St. Philip had a marvellous devotion to Him, and the Holy Ghost worked wonders in St. Philip ... X—— has actually gone off to Spain *on purpose* to see the eclipse there. Is it not extraordinary? I can't understand how anyone who has given himself to God could take such interest in anything except what was for God's greater glory.* But we must not judge him, and perhaps I am wrong in saying this about

---

* It must be remembered that Clare was only seventeen when she made this rather severe criticism.

him. I hope you have as much devotion as you used to have to the Sacred Heart. Do you remember two years ago?... Let us ask St. Clare that we may never leave it, and that she may intercede and bring us nearer to it every day. Time passes so swiftly—may it bring us nearer and nearer to God. Alas! what a subject of humiliation it is to think how few actions we do *merely* and *entirely* from the love of God, with what mixed motives we do even our good actions! So let us ask St. Francis to obtain for us a great *purity of heart;* then will come purity of thought, purity of action; then indeed all things will be done purely for God's glory and His love. I very seldom write to any one, not only because I have no time, but because I think, as Father Faber says, letter-writing is such a great destroyer of spirituality. Of course this does not refer to when I write to you, as we generally speak about spiritual things, and it is far the most interesting subject, after all. I wonder where we shall meet again? I envy you those evenings you talk of at Ince when you go out of doors. I think Nature is never so beautiful as then; all is so calm and peaceful, the beauty and silence of it all comes over one like a dream. 'Nature always looks most pleased with herself in the evening.' Write soon. I send my best love to Maymie and Tizzie."

CHAPTER III.

CLARE's prognostications were not fulfilled; and a month later, early in August, she started with her father for Ince Blundell. This visit is thus described by Clare's friend N——, to whom most of her letters were written, and who takes the account entirely from a journal kept by her at the time of her friend's visit to Ince Blundell:

"How well I remember her visit to Ince Blundell! We had been expecting Uncle John, but had no idea he was going to bring Clare with him, till two days before, when he wrote to announce it. The news seemed almost too good to be true. What plans we made! What excursions we were going to undertake together! All the old jokes were to be revived; there was nothing in the old times, already nearly three years old—an eternity in those days—which was not going to be repeated with variations. In fact, there was no end to the castles in the air; and through it all there was the odd sensation—perhaps misgiving,—shall we find each other changed? Shall we be all that we were to each other? and a thousand other vague feelings one can hardly give a name to. At last the day arrived. How well I remember the very room we were sitting in, the time of day, and, at last, Clare's arrival! When the general excitement had subsided a little, we went up together to show her her room,—the room close to mine, where we were to be so happy together. Then, for the first time, we began to talk, and I to take a good look at her. As

she was then I shall remember her all my life—exactly as
she stood in her brown dress, a dress which meant nothing,
as was the nature of all Clare's gowns, but was merely the
simplest of coverings to a body which looked already
less body than soul. Clare was then seventeen and a
half, that is to say, what it is the fashion to call 'out,'
launched into society; but nothing could look less like
a young lady prepared to take that desperate plunge
than the slight girlish figure which I see so plainly before me when I shut my eyes and call back that beloved
past. I remember the first impression was, 'How beautiful she is! how much better looking than I expected
to find her!' I suppose it was the flush of excitement
of arriving which for a moment gave her ordinarily pale
cheeks a slight momentary flush, and added to the lus-
tre of her deep brown eyes. It was indeed a face which
nobody having once seen would quickly forget; not on
account of the regularity of features, but because of the
ever-varying expression, which changed a hundred
times in the course of a minute, and which lent it a
matchless charm, her eyes especially dilating with interest when any deed of heroism was spoken of, or rip-
pling with brightest laughter when anything amused her.
There was nothing of the austere devotee about her, in
her face or expression, any more than in her character.
If there was any harshness about her it only displayed
itself, or rather was wreaked upon her own delicate
frame, which in her moments of glee she used to amuse
herself by calling every sort of ridiculous and abusive
name; but to all around she was invariable in her gen-
tleness and charity. To return to that memorable day.

How much we had to say to each other, and as in all friendships after absence—because nobody, however sincere, can exactly express their very selves in a letter—how much there was to learn about each other! And then I discovered that what I vaguely suspected had indeed taken place. We had parted the greatest friends, almost equals; but now I saw she was not only miles ahead of me in every way, but she was in a different hemisphere. It made no difference to our friendship, rather it deepened it, but henceforth it was as that of the master and his disciple. The next few days I count amongst the most perfectly happy of my life. Little by little I drew from her the history of her life in the interval since we parted; but it was not so much in the meagre detail of a life which had been so peculiarly uneventful, spent almost entirely within four walls, but in the tone of her mind, in the way she treated every subject, in her plans for the future, that I discovered how entirely God had taken possession of a heart in which He was now First and Only. I must acknowledge that it was not without a desperate pang that I found out, first in one way, then in another, how Clare had become indifferent to, or had gradually detached herself from pleasures innocent, indeed, but still not wholly for God or of God—pleasures to which I clung with all my human heart. I remember at last frantically reproaching her with caring for nothing on earth, for giving up a thousand things which she had once held dear. Our life together had been such a delightful one, so full of impossible but glorious dreams, so full, so complete. But it was not to be. Clare had passed by these, but she had not stopped, and was now beginning that painful, terrible ascent in which the devout soul, supported by her Divine Spouse, follows again with Him the road to Calvary, and which ended only with her death in the Convent of Amiens. There were times, however, when Clare was perfectly happy—nay, more, radiant and transformed,—and that was in the presence of the Blessed Sacrament. We used to go in the evening, when everybody was engaged, and there was least likelihood of interruption. She began always with a visit to the Altar of Our Lady, where she used to recite the Rosary of the Seven Dolors,—to get it over, she used to say laughingly. Not that she had not the very greatest devotion to Our Lady, but because she knew by experience that once she found herself at the feet of Our Lord in the Sacrament of His love, it was an absolute impossibility to her to tear herself away till it was time to leave altogether. This done, she used to go and prostrate herself at the steps of the sanctuary, and pour out her whole heart and soul *aloud:* for it was impossible for her to keep in or suppress what she felt of love, praise, or adoration of Him who was indeed her life, her love, her joy, her all in all. Never shall I forget the way she *rejoiced* in the Blessed Sacrament. It was as if it were something newly come to her with the joy of a great surprise; something, or rather some one, of whom she had only just learnt all the delight and the charm. Truly she could say with the prophet, ' The children of men shall put their trust under the covert of Thy wings; they shall be inebriated with the plenty of Thy House, and Thou shalt make them drink of the torrent of Thy pleasure.' Our Lord seemed—in compensation, perhaps, for the dreariness and many sorrows of her life—to have given her a rapturous happiness and joy in His presence, such as one hardly likes to describe as vividly as one remembers it, for fear of its being misunderstood. Perhaps this supernatural joy in the Blessed Sacrament was only, or partly, the result (as Father Faber, in one of his books, tells us to expect it) of the continual mortifications and austerities she was in the habit of practising.* Her love of mortification was such that nothing she saw, or came across, failed to suggest some means of torturing or annoying her unfortunate body. How well I remember one day, when we were returning from a village in the neighborhood, we happened to be passing through a stubble field, and breaking off suddenly from what she had been talking about, she cried, 'I have a splendid idea! Supposing we take off our shoes and stockings, and walk barefoot through the stubble field?' It was no sooner said than done; and I can see now the calm enjoyment with which Clare walked up and down those cruel many-bristling thorns (followed by the sympathetic shrieks of her cowardly companion, who very soon resumed shoes and stockings) till at last she was obliged to succumb and allow the poor bleeding feet to be tied up. Another day we came across a flourishing family of nettles, and she instantly seized hold of a large bunch in order to discipline herself with them at leisure on her return home. Another favorite

* "Mortification, and especially bodily mortification, is the shortest way to cheerfulness and supernatural joy."—Spiritual Conf., p. 332.

mortification of hers was to wait, after she got into bed, till she was beginning to feel thoroughly warm and comfortable, and then springing out of bed to spend half-an-hour prostrate on the ground in prayer, often with arms extended, in order to add the discomfort of the posture to the other mortifications. On Thursdays, she used constantly to prolong this prayer till far into the night, in union with the prayer of Our Lord in the Garden. This she did with the special intention of assisting souls in their agony; indeed, it was for this, and for another which was equally dear to her—the conversion of sinners,—that all her actions were offered up. She had the tenderest love and devotion to the Holy Souls, but she used to say she *knew* they were all right; and so though they were continually remembered in her prayers, yet the other seemed to be the motive which was most constantly present with her, and was ever spurring her on to fresh exertions. It was not, however, in exterior mortification, only that Clare eclipsed everybody that I ever saw or knew. She was much too well versed in the science of the Saints not to know that if God is pleased with the self-inflicted sufferings of souls united to Him in love and desire of expiation, He is still more pleased with those interior mortifications which attack the very seat and origin of evil within us, and enable us, by His grace, to become triumphant masters, not only of our flesh (as in the case of exterior mortification), but of our very wills and souls. Clare was naturally of an indolent disposition. The Southern blood in her veins, which showed too clearly in her face, was also strongly marked in her disposition. With this characteristic she had another, and this was that she was by nature what the French would call *d'un caractère vif*—quick, easily roused, I cannot say to anger, as nobody that ever saw Clare, though they might have seen the blood rising quickly to her cheek, could ever have seen more, unless in those cases in which we are told we may be angry and sin not. Still the grace of God enabled her to overcome so perfectly these weaknesses, that nobody who knew her, especially in those days of which I am speaking, would ever have suspected their existence. One means she had discovered, both of mortifying herself interiorly and of curing herself of defects whose magnitude she was ever exaggerating, was that of holding a Chapter, or, in other words, imitating the religious observance common to a great many Orders of making a public confession of faults.* How well I remember the satisfaction she used to take in unearthing and, as it were, running to ground all those little weaknesses into which even the best amongst us sometimes fall, but which it is one of the chief objects of life with most, having committed them, to conceal from the eyes of others. In this case what made her humility even more striking was that her elected Father Confessor was much younger than herself, and naturally inclined, as she must have been perfectly aware, to make a heroine of her, so that she had all the greater merit in humbling herself before him. I feel it would give a very false idea of Clare, as she was at this period of her

* Public, in the sense of not being made to a confessor, or under the seal of confession.

life, if one represented her simply as saying her prayers all day, and spending her time in trampling her nature under foot. Besides this side of her character she had another very human, bright, and lovable one. She used at times to have what she called her "lazy days," when she used to get hold of some exciting book, and sit curled up on a sofa half the day reading it—perfectly happy if she got one or two others she cared for to share the pleasure by reading it with them. Books, like every other occupation, lost half their interest to her if she could not talk them over with her friends, and share the interest with them. In this manner I remember we got through 'Uncle Tom's Cabin' in half-a-dozen summer days. She loved talking about books and authors, in fact, her tastes were thoroughly literary. One of her heroines in that way was Madame de Stael. She used always to lament so that a woman of such talents, with such convincing power of language, and, above all, so enthusiastic for everything great and elevated, should not have been a Catholic. She was very fond of quoting that wonderful saying of her's, '*Le mystère de l'existence c'est le rapport entre nos erreurs et nos peines.*' At last Clare's visit drew to a close. A few days before she was to leave everybody happened to be dining out, and we had—rare occurrence—the whole house to ourselves. I remember this prospect of an uninterrupted *tête-à-tête* was one we thoroughly enjoyed. We discussed how we should spend it; whether we should sit out in the garden or spend it over our books, when Clare suggested, 'Supposing we assemble all the servants in the schoolroom; first we will have the Rosary before the statue of Our Lady, then I will speak to them about the love of God for sinners, etc.' I shall always regret that with truly British *mauvaise honte* I implored her to give up this wild (for so it seemed to me) idea. I can now see Clare's face, with its bright, earnest look as she answered my objections. 'How it would be so easy—quite impossible to break down, etc.' A few days after and Clare left Ince. We never met again."

CHAPTER IV.

ABOUT this date (the autumn of 1860) a fresh phase, or rather we might say, a further development, of Clare's spiritual life seems to have taken place. We have seen with what fervor she had given herself up to the service of God—heart, soul, desires, words,—there was nothing she kept back. Yet, as He condescends to call Himself a jealous God, He continued to ask for more; and this holy soul, responding to the voice of her Divine Spouse, gave more, and yet more.

To those who knew her well this change was very apparent. Her whole being seemed to grow in the hands of God. Till now she had been a child with the weakness of a child—its impulses and its impetuosities, its likes and its dislikes,—but in the year that followed (the most important year of a girl's life, that between seventeen and eighteen) all these characteristics of childhood gave way before a higher, holier state of being. Like the valiant woman of the Bible, " She had put out her hand to strong things, her fingers had taken hold of the spindle." Each day she appeared to make fresh progress in virtue. She was never tired of repeating the beautiful words of St. Francis, " Let us *begin* to serve the Lord our God, for hitherto we have made very little progress." And these words so constantly on her lips, and even more deeply implanted in her heart, were ever urging her on to fresh efforts in His service.

She felt that God was calling her to higher things; and with the whole fervor of her soul she responded, turning, as it were, towards Him, and renouncing for His sake her dearest affections—mortifying each thought, and will, and inclination, and rejoicing with the greatest ardor at suffering something for His sake.

Everything now appeared to pall upon her which was not for God and for Him alone. Till now she had always taken the greatest pleasure in reading; poetry especially was her delight, and it had been the one recreation which she had allowed herself, and she had indulged in it freely. But the time had come when she felt herself called upon to renounce even this. Little by little she gave up everything in the shape of profane literature. Shelley, Byron, all the poets she had taken greatest delight in, and who, by their glowing words and lively descriptions, appealed in a special manner to an ardent soul like hers—which was by nature so keenly alive to everything melancholy, wild, or heroic—all were given up. That page of her life was closed. She felt these things did not lead her to God. Her studies were now of another nature, and with her accustomed energy she threw herself into the study of what has been well called, the science of the saints. She had always been a great reader of lives of saints, and other spiritual works, and from a child had been familiar with the works of Rodrigues, St. Francis of Sales, Faber, Newman, and innumerable other holy writers; and it was to these she turned now for that spiritual nourishment which her soul required. In her letters (of which a good many have been preserved, written about this time) constant mention is made of the books she has been, or is, reading. In one place she writes:

"You should read St. Ignatius's 'Spiritual Exercises.' It is a most glorious work—meditations they are by St. Ignatius. It was that book which he took so many years in compiling, which made St. Ignatius such a wonderful saint; in fact, it made all the Jesuit saints. And there is another magnificent book I am very fond of also, called 'Spiritual Doctrine,' by Lallemant. It is most suggestive, and meant for those who aim high."

Another great interest of hers at this time was the study of Latin, which she had already begun the previous year. She had, as we have seen, long made up her mind to join the Poor Clares, by whom she knew the Divine Office was daily recited; she therefore longed to prepare herself for this great privilege by becoming acquainted with the language of the Church (in which it is always said), so as to enter more completely into the spirit and meaning of the holy words.

But if we thus enter into detail about the interests and occupation of her leisure moments, it is only to throw greater light upon what we may call the inner purpose and meaning of Clare's life. This was her love of prayer—or in other words, her union with God. Prayer was the occupation of her life, or as her sister described it in a little sketch which was written at the request of the Community at Amiens, it was "the breath of her soul." Study, spiritual lectures, all else were but as oil to the flame which, as a faithful virgin, she burnt day and night before her Beloved. Her prayers might be said to be continual; whenever she could, she escaped from the house to go and spend hours before the Blessed Sacrament, there to kneel entranced in the presence of Him who remains forever a victim of love upon our altars. The smaller, the poorer, the more neglected the chapel, the better; Jesus was there —it was enough. What she loved best was to kneel among the poor at the bottom of the chapel, too glad if she were mistaken for one of those favored children of the Lord. If by any accident the church door was locked, it was the greatest happiness to her to kneel on the steps of the entrance. There, with her head leaning against the door, which alone separated her from the dwelling of her only love, she would (as her sisters witnessed) pour forth her soul in passionate love and praise of Jesus in the Blessed Sacrament, and before turning to go away would tenderly kiss the door which separated her from Him.

No one who had ever seen her receiving Holy Communion would ever forget the sight. After returning to her place she remained absolutely absorbed in God; she was insensible to any outside sight or distraction. Truly, in looking at her, one might be reminded of the verse in the Canticle, "My Beloved to me and I to Him who feedeth among the lilies." To quote again from the same life:

"Nothing could interrupt her union with God, or her exercises of piety (not even the headaches she suffered from, which were sometimes so violent as to cause involuntary tears to stream from her eyes); often, after her bedtime, she would spend long hours kneeling at the foot of her bed, and very often her prayers were prolonged far into the night. One night I happened to awake, and heard the clock strike twelve ; Clare was still in the midst of her prayers, and showed no signs of concluding them. 'Do get up,' I said to her; 'it is quite time for you to get some rest; it is late, and in the morning you will be worn out.' 'Do you think so?' she said; 'I thought I had just begun, I did not know it was late.' Often when awaking at night she would return without effort to her prayers, as a person, obliged for a moment to leave her work, goes back naturally to resume it when the interruption is over ... What shall I say to you, Reverend Mother, of her love for the Blessed Sacrament? It was, as you well know, her life's occupation, or rather her life itself ... She would never pass over the smallest irreverence committed in the presence of the Blessed Sacrament by either her brothers or sisters, yet there was no bitterness in this holy zeal, alienating while it wounds. As Jesus Christ deigns to become a Victim for the love of us in the Blessed Sacrament, and she also aspired to the same title, it would be impossible for me to say to what length her spirit of penance and the practice of voluntary mortifications led her. Besides the use of the hair-shirt, with which she was familiar, she was accustomed to rub herself with nettles ; and on several occasions when walking in the country she took off shoes and stockings and walked barefoot among the briars and thorns, and on another occasion in a stubble field, where the corn was newly cut. She used always to say her greatest misery was having to eat ; and she would often, if she could, put away the food that was sent up for her meals in order to give it away to the poor."

In Clare's letters she makes continual allusion to the comfort and joy she derives from prayer, and is never tired—always in the gentlest and humblest fashion—of recommending the practice of it to her correspondents. In a letter written about this time to a dear friend, she says:

"What a comfort that God is everywhere, and always ready to hear you and comfort you wherever you are; and that when no one understands you, and when your real secret heart is undisclosed to anyone, *He* always understands, and in every difficulty will never fail you! I should fancy that ejaculatory prayer would be a great help to you. Years ago Herbert advised me to practice the habit of ejaculatory prayer. Make a resolution when you rise in the morning to offer up your heart to God five times during the day, and then in the evening examine yourself if you have done so, and if you persevere in this during the month, you have no idea how much good it will have done you—how it will give a spiritual tone to your whole mind, and how it will gain you the gift of the sense of God's continual Presence. I know it has done much for me. I *hope* and trust I do not appear to be preaching. I suppose you must often feel sick of the world, you must often feel that you crave for something greater, higher, to satisfy you, than what the world can offer you. What heroic creatures the saints were; after all, they are the only true heroes the world has ever seen. I often think that there is perhaps an immense deal of stuff of which heroism is made in women's hearts, but that conventionalism, and its laws, crushes and beats it down."

Besides the practice of mental prayer, in which Clare was so great a proficient, there were certain vocal prayers to which she had the greatest devotion. She never failed to say the Rosary of Our Lady of Seven Dolors daily, and her love of the Souls in Purgatory found its vent in great devotion to Indulgenced Prayers. Chief among these was the Gloria Patri. She seemed specially drawn to the use of this prayer, and was never tired of repeating it; and she used to love, when she found herself alone in the chapel, to say it with profound prostration at the holy Names, stopping a long time over each one. Another devotion she loved was that of saying the six Our Fathers, Hail Marys, and Glorias with her arms extended in the shape of a cross. This prayer fulfilled both her fondest wishes by combining prayer and penance.

CHAPTER V.

CLARE'S visit to Ince Blundell over, her life again resumed its usual routine. From that time to the following spring she only left London on two occasions to visit her friends in the country for a few days at a time. Her letters meanwhile give us a vivid insight into her inner history, ever of greater interest than the one known to the world at large—which in her case was singularly devoid of incident. The first letter we have of Clare's is dated within a few days of her return to London. It is to her friend N——.

"Who is with us? *Benedicamus Domino.** I was delighted to receive your letter this morning. I don't think you can miss me more than I do you. Try and fight against your unfortunate *dumps*. It is a little trial and cross which our dear Lord sends you in order that you may offer it up to His Sacred Heart. Your very feeling of weariness, if you offer it up to His loving Heart, will be the means of adding fresh jewels to your crown. How happy we were before the Blessed Sacrament a few days ago! I wish I was prostrate before His altar now. Hélas!—We arrived here yesterday evening at 10 o'clock; the whole time in the train I was reading the 'Following of Christ' you gave me, and meditating upon it ... Please try for

* Clare had made an agreement with her friend N—— that all her letters to her should begin with this greeting. The answer, of course, was, *Deo Gratias*.

my sake to be as cheerful as you can. Perhaps behind the clouds is the sun still shining. This is a sad world, is it not? It is sin which has made it so sad; and it is so made up of meetings and partings. Oh, how good God is in all this! Don't you see, dear, it is all because He fears that we shall set too much value on this poor world? Adieu! My best love to Maymie. May God and His holy angels ever watch over you and protect you and guard you. May you never leave the Sacred Heart, in which I am your loving cousin,

"CLARE."

A few weeks later she writes again to the same correspondent:

"It is raining so awfully, and the day looks so hopelessly dreary that I think there is no chance of our taking a walk, I therefore sit down to write you a long letter. I am sorry —— is suffering so much. I hear of her everywhere from everyone. I will pray for her, and will write her a letter to ask her to give me an account of her dear self . . . I hope you often pray for me when you are prostrate in the sanctuary before the Blessed Sacrament. Jesus should be our only joy and happiness here, as He will be our everlasting joy and happiness in our eternal home. I have finished the life of our sweet and angel Mother. It took more even than the book you gave me for it could contain; when you come here I will show it to you. Father —— preached such a beautiful sermon last Sunday. Has he written since I left Ince, to you? Uncle Dick is very fond of him, and says he is a very holy, spiritual man, and that we could not do better than trust him implicitly. We have not even yet given the treat to the children of the Home. What a pity you do not come in November! I shall never see you again, dear N——. We must hope to see each other in Heaven, but we must work hard to get there. Heaven cannot be gained without a struggle, and we have each of us got our crosses to carry; and we must carry them with a cheerful heart, and embrace every trial as a means to a great end. I know you have many little trials to bear from others, and also from your own natural character and disposition. It is your very thoughtfulness of mind, etc., which makes you feel so low-spirited and weary. Fight against it as long as you live. Never give way to discouragement at anything. Courage, St. Teresa says, is necessary for a person who is striving at perfection; and when you feel lonely, and because I know often in the midst of many there is loneliness—loneliness of heart, of sympathy—offer that up to the Sacred Heart. He knows you, and sees to the very depth of your heart, because He is a Man-God. He can sympathize, He can console as no other can. But perhaps I am preaching too much, and am wearying you, which I should be so sorry to do. I liked very much your last letter, especially what you said about the sea. I am growing awfully fond of the true Cross! I wish it was mine! Pray very much for me that God's Holy Will may be done in all things. I will do the same for you. Have I not written you a long letter?"

Shortly afterwards she writes again to the same friend:

"I wrote you a long letter on All Saints, but had no time to finish it, and now I find it too stale to send you, so begin another at Maiden Erlegh, where I arrived yesterday evening. How kind of you to send me that MS., and how like your own dear self to send me anything at all! I thank you exceedingly for it, and shall prize it as a present from my dearest old cousin. I thank you also immensely for offering up Holy Communion for me on the feast of All Saints. I did not forget you on that glorious Festa, and I asked the Father Francis and Mother Clare to take you specially under their protection. Surely they could not refuse anything to however unworthy the creature who asked them on that glorious day. How empty Purgatory must look after all the prayers yesterday! Let us every day during this month beg St. Francis and St. Clare to do all they can to get a soul out of Purgatory—say the soul most devoted to the Seven Dolors, and nearest its release. I will not forget to give you a portrait of my disgusting self, and I will willingly leave you my story. I am writing out, in a sort of MS., various things for you, viz., sayings from the saints and different prayers to St. Francis and St. Clare of my own composition, with a few more other prayers from the same quarter. I intend also copying some prayers which I think particularly beautiful. I hope you will care for them. I don't indeed deserve all you say about me in your letter. I often grieve that I have not been always as gentle and kind as I ought to have been towards you. What impatience have I not often shown in my conversation! You remember, I dare say, to what I allude. I light the lamp here before the Blessed Sacrament. They have got such a delicious little chapel. I do indeed wish with you that we could hold a Chapter together as in days past. Was it not good fun, besides being improving to our souls! I am so delighted, *enchanted*, that you really think it is your vocation to be a poor Clare. Keep to it, and keep to it in the *sanctuary of your heart*. Speak only to God about it, and to Him Who holds the place of God. It is a great treasure which you must keep silently and lovingly until the time comes when I shall see you in our Mother's convent singing the praises of Him to Whom alone is honor and praise everlasting."

Whilst Clare was staying with her friends at Maiden Erlegh, the following singular incident occurred. She was kneeling one day in the chapel, as usual, immersed in prayer, when she happened to lift her eyes to the altar. She had thought herself alone, and so was astonished to see a hand stretched from behind the tabernacle and moving noiselessly among the flowers on each side of it. On looking further, she noticed that the hand was busily occupied in re-arranging the flowers, pulling out and rejecting those that were faded. Clare, on leaving the chapel, instantly asked Miss Plowden and her sisters if any of them had been behind the altar at the time, and was answered in the negative. They were thus forced to conclude that the singular appearance was sent to teach them the lesson that our Lord loves to see beauty and order reigning in His temple and in " the place where His glory dwelleth."

A little later, she writes from the same place:

"Now for a long letter to you in answer to yours of Tuesday. I will pray for —— indeed. I am so very sorry to hear such a bad account of her. You will be glad to hear Teresa's cough is better—that is, at least, what I hear from Montague Square. Now dear N——, I will get your letter from the depths of my pocket, and will answer your questions by giving you my humble opinion. First, do not worry and trouble yourself about the doubts you speak of on the subject of your religious vocation. I can't say whether you have one or not, God only knows; but pray earnestly and humbly to God to show you His will in regard to your future state. Never omit this prayer—let it be your *daily* prayer. These doubts of yours may, or may not, be temptations. If they are temptations, don't flatter the devil by bothering yourself about them. After all, the great thing you have to look to is to do God's will in your present state of life. Don't trouble yourself so much about the future. Your path is plainly marked out for you for some years. Your work is to be obedient, patient, humble, and gentle to all, and to keep as much as you can in God's presence. If you do all this, God will reward you by showing you His will about your state of life. That state of life which you think will help you best to Heaven—that state of life is yours. What do you think? Will a vocation in the world help you best to love God, and obtain your end—Heaven, or a vocation to Religion? *I* think that this latter life will be best for you, when you tell me that when you enter society and speak of worldly things you care less for God. Often ask yourself, 'Which will help me *best* to Heaven? Which will help me best to love God?' If you can answer this, God's will is clear. I think, dear N——, that you must pray a great deal that God may give you a constant sense of His presence. Then the world's esteem and applause will be nothing to you, and you will feel how foolish it is to care for anyone's esteem but God's. Whenever your mother wishes you to go into society, of course you must obey, and *cheerfully* too ; but remember that God is with you, particularly at such times, and offer up your heart and actions to Him, and ask Him to have mercy on you. But when she does not express any wish about it, *then* if you find worldly conversation and worldly society does not help you to God, *don't* seek it, and do not, darling, be discouraged in the least at your liking of the world. Speak to Our Lord about it, when you visit Him in His Adorable Sacrament, and do not forget every day to offer up that heart of yours to His Sacred Heart."

Another correspondent of Clare's, Father Edmund Vaughan, who besides being her uncle, had two other claims on her confidence, being also her godfather and her director, receives a letter from her, of about this date (December, 1860). It contains the first mention of her wishes and plans as regards the carrying out of her religious vocation. We shall see later on how soon these desires were to meet with their fulfilment.

"I am writing this epistle merely to extract a letter from you, so please do not forget this. I am longing to be a Poor Clare. God alone knows *how I long*. Papa hardly thinks I am strong enough for such an Order, and I am dreadfully afraid he will not let me go at

Easter, as he promised me some time ago. I myself believe I shall never be strong until I am a Poor Clare, and for this reason, that I shall never be happy until then. Reason, however, is ever ready to chime in with our wishes, so I suppose not much confidence can be placed in *that*. I am going to make a Novena that, if it be God's will, I may enter the Poor Clares the Friday in Easter week. The Novena begins next Thursday; I hope you will not forget me. I shall try what power there is in prayer! I always expect an immensity of trial and suffering when I am a nun; were it only for that, no wonder nuns are happy! Pain gives me a great deal of happiness; one feels so *thoroughly* belonging more to God, because we know His hand is upon us. Oh, what does anything matter so that we only become more like that Heart which was once so full of sorrow; that Heart abandoned by all, even by God Himself! . . . But this sounds as if I were going to preach, so I will stop instantly. I have just finished reading the life of St. Colette, the great Reformer of the Franciscans. There is a great difference between the Seraphic Mother, St. Clare, and the glorious Reformer, St. Colette: at least I mean that from her birth St. Colette's will and character seem *naturally* so immensely firm and strong, and so suited, inasmuch as a woman can be suited, for such an arduous and difficult mission; and then she had a much sterner spirit than St. Clare, there seems to have been more of a woman's gentle feeling combined with her natural devotedness of heart and generosity and firmness of purpose; and when the grace of God so wondrously got possession of such a heart, and reigned there and consumed everything earthly in it, *then* what a seraph of love she became! Her passionate burning love for Our Lord, and her character also is like St. Mary Magdalene (penitent), so it appears to me, while St. Mary of Egypt represents St. Colette. I take such interest in the lives of saints. They teach so much about God, and each time they are read we learn something fresh from them. St. Francis's life in this respect is inexhaustible. How wonderful poor weak man can become with the strength of the grace of God! I am anxious to read the life of St. Alphonsus, which I have not yet done. I have been feeling often lately heavy and gloomy in mind, and the devil is busy with his temptations. This is partly the reason I have been so long writing to you. I beg of you to pray for me. I have a particular claim on your prayers, as you are my godfather. I often say to Our Lord, 'Why hast Thou done this? Govern, O Lord, the thing which Thou hast created.' It is from St. Augustine, as of course you know. I hope your Mission did a great deal of good. I heard, the other day, that Father Coffin is the Confessor Extraordinary of the Poor Clares. I hope this is true ... Is it not a comfort that Joe is professed! There is no danger now of his coming out, *Deo Gratias!* I have indeed written a long letter; I hope I have not tired you with it. What a glorious saint was St. Francis (I really must say *one* word more about him); he was like a comet amongst the bright stars of his Order. St. Francis, pray for us!"

Christmas was always a time of special love and rejoicing to Clare, and so as this beloved Feast comes round, she writes the following beautiful letter to her usual correspondent:

"I wish you a very happy Christmas, 'for I bring you tidings of great joy. This day is born to you a Saviour.' I wish you such intense joy and peace—a joy that the world cannot understand, and a peace that surpasses all understanding. He has indeed come to bring peace to men of good will. Can I trust you with a secret, so that you will not tell it to *any* living soul? If you will promise me that you will not disclose it, on any account, to anyone, I will tell it to you in my next letter. Is there any chance of your coming up to London next year? How are you, my darling? Write and give an account of yourself! I think Teresa's cough is a little better, notwithstanding the cold weather. I went to the Oratory the other day, and afterwards to see Miss Mereweather. I am sure you will be delighted to hear that her maid, Ann, has just become a Catholic, and she is so happy, and it is such a comfort to Miss Mereweather. How is Tizzie? When you write to me please place this letter before your visage, and answer all the questions contained therein ... I am afraid you will find it very dull when your papa and mamma leave for Lulworth. Never mind, dear N——, you know that you can offer it up to the Sacred Heart of our dear Lord. Let us do all we can this month, especially to love and serve the little King who has done so much out of love for us. Love this little Child, for He is exceedingly to be loved. 'Come, then, let us love the Babe of Bethlehem,' is the enraptured cry of our beloved Father Francis. I went to midnight Mass at Farm Street. It was glorious; but the misery was not to have been able to go to Holy Communion there, as it is not allowed in London. I suppose you had that happiness at home, in your delicious church. I have got a particular love for your church. There is something so grand and wide about it; I like the Roman style so much ... We are trying to make a Christmas tree for the children at the Home, but we have not bought the tree, and have a very few *rubbishy things* to put on it when we do get it. Now you told me some time ago that Uncle Tom had given you thirteen shillings for the poor children. I wish you would send it for them in your next letter, as no one has got *a penny* to buy the tree and presents, and that will help immensely. You could send it in stamps. Now, my darling, farewell."

We suppose her friend's asseverations were considered satisfactory. At least we find soon after the following letter was received:

"Many thanks for your letter, which I received a few days ago. My secret is that I am to go to the Poor Clares at Bayswater, at Easter. Papa has promised me. I don't want it to be known until I am gone. The Friday in Easter week I have chosen to enter, it being dedicated to the Sacred Heart. Get prayers for me, please, and you yourself pray for me like wildfire, but do not say for what intention you get the prayers. I hope you will in time join me, and we will help each other to love God immensely, and with our whole hearts. I must now tell you about the Christmas tree for the poor children of the Home, which went off with great *éclat* last Monday. I wish you had been there to have seen their intense eagerness and joy. Papa and

Mary go to Lulworth on Monday, so I shall be left in comparative solitude, except for my dear companions— my books,—which are always agreeable and interesting. I have just been reading the life of Blessed Peter Claver. Such a gloriously heroic saint, who devoted his entire life to the service of the negroes—a life of forty years! I enjoy immensely reading saints' lives. They are 'like heroes of romance, so gracefully, so nobly, so royally do they bear themselves; their actions are as beautiful as fiction, yet as real as facts.' I shall be delighted to leave our children of the Home to you, dearest, and it will be very jolly if you could collect enough to give them a treat yearly. Don't you think my secret *gloriously* magnificent for me? I am always thinking of it."

In another very characteristic letter, which she writes to an intimate friend a good deal younger than herself, she says:

"I am so *very* glad that you are always kind and gentle and considerate to those under you—I mean the servants. A—— told me this. I have *such* horror of haughtiness to servants. As if we were not made of the same dust! I always make it a particular point to be kind to the so-called lower class . . . Life is short; let us make the best of every opportunity to suffer and work for our Divine Master. Talk a great deal to the Sacred Heart about your desire of belonging entirely to Him. I wanted to talk to you about Lent, and what we may do for our beloved Lord, as we cannot fast. I will think of some penance—interior,—and then write and tell you. Please do the same for me."

CHAPTER VI.

THE history of Clare's vocation might be said to be the history of her life. As other children learn fairly tales, legends, stories of all kinds at their mother's knee, so Clare loved to hear, even as her mother loved to tell her, stories of the saints—of their wonderful heroism, their dauntless courage, their willing sacrifice of joy, happiness, life itself, in the service of their Master.

The story of her own particular patron saint, St. Clare, was chief favorite among these. Clare was never tired of hearing about that heroic servant of God, and her mother, who had no dearer wish than that she should become a nun, used laughingly to call her her little "Poor Clare." Though so early deprived by death of her beloved mother, the seed had been sown, and it fell on fruitful soil. At the great moment of her First Communion, she was inspired to make a vow of perpetual virginity; and from that moment it is not too much to say that Clare never for an instant wavered in her determination, at the very earliest possible occasion, to devote herself to the service of God in the Religious life. Some people will only see in the above action a dangerous precedent which no youthful fervor could justify, and in ordinary cases no doubt they would be right. On the other hand, who can deny that God sometimes attracts souls and leads them by extraordinary ways? No one could have read, even so far, the history of Clare's life, without seeing that she was no ordinary child. At the age of twelve, sorrow and grace had done their work in her soul, she had learnt the terrible lesson that some learn late in life; some spend all their time in learning, and yet hardly fully understand, to the last, that "all is vanity" except loving and serving God.

What time and experience do for most people, the sharp sword of anguish did for Clare. From the moment of her mother's death, life—or at least everything that made life desirable—was ended for this loving, faithful child. She never knew afterwards what it was to be happy, and her only solace was working for others, and forwarding the interests of her beloved Lord and Master in the world. All her prayers and works of penance were directed to this end—the salvation of sinners, intercession for the souls in Purgatory,—whatever objects we know through faith to be the interests of the loving Heart of Jesus, she made hers also. Nor were the poor, the special children of His love, forgotten. It is not too much to say of Clare that she had a passionate love of Poverty. It was the master passion of her dear St. Francis; and with that characteristic enthusiasm which was such a prominent feature of her character, from the moment she made up her mind to become a Poor Clare, she adopted and made her very own all the beautiful traditions and devotions of that most glorious saint, and, as far as she could, made his very spirit hers. She was never tired of talking of this beautiful Poverty of St Francis, his *dama Povertà* to whom he was mystically espoused, and for whose sake he had so joyfully renounced all things, and been counted as a madman. But Clare was not satisfied in imitating her holy model in words only. Like him she rejoiced in serving the poor, in depriving herself of all she had for them, and in treating herself on all possible opportunities as their equal, nay, their inferior. Her greatest joy was to save up what was intended for her own meals for them, and when she had no money to give them, she joyfully parted with any little treasure she had, even to her very beads and crucifix. Anything she could call her own, she longed not only to share with them, but to deprive herself utterly of, for their benefit. We cannot do better than quote again from the letter written by her sister on this subject. She says:

"We had a school not far from us, in London, in the Parish of Westminster, and to go there was one of Clare's chief pleasures. She always singled out the most wretched and repulsive-looking child amongst them, and on this child would lavish all her care and attention. It was to him that she loved to talk about our dear Lord and His Mother, for whom it is needless to say she had a special devotion. Shortly before her departure for Amiens, Clare wished to give a splendid feast to her children of the Ragged School. She assembled them accordingly in a large room, serving them at dinner with her own hands, and standing as their humble servant behind their chairs; afterwards she distributed amongst them and their families great numbers of rosaries, as a last pledge of her love for the Mother of God."

The Ragged School was, as we have seen, in her

thoughts to the last, and in leaving the world she made provision for it by bequeathing the care of providing it with a yearly treat to her most intimate friend. To be poor, or friendless, or afflicted, was to insure a welcome from Clare. Though, as a rule, she avoided company, and it was a real effort to her to go down to the drawing-room to receive visitors, if she was told that a poor person wished to see her, she lost not a moment in going to him. On one occasion (one of her sisters happening to be present) a Jesuit lay-brother came to the house to beg. This being a visitor after Clare's own heart, having the two things she loved best (holiness and poverty) to recommend him, she conversed freely for some time with him. On leaving, he thanked her for her kindness, and said that it was too much condescension on the part of a grand young lady like her to talk so familiarly to a poor ignorant man, a servant of the servants of God. "A grand lady!" she cried. "What can you be thinking of? I am nothing but a poor person myself, and I shall never be happy till I have given up everything and embraced the Poverty of St. Francis."

To some it may be a cause of astonishment that with her love of the poor, and the special attraction she always manifested for the conversion of sinners, Clare should have chosen to join a contemplative rather than an active Order. To Clare, however, this difficulty never presented itself. She had no hesitation; God called her to the more perfect way; she heard His voice in her soul, and obeyed. But if it had been urged upon her that by serving Christ in the persons of His poor as a Sister of Charity, or working for the reclamation of sinners as a Good Shepherd nun, she would be more certain of pleasing Him and accomplishing His Divine Will on earth, she would have made the same answer as the Church has made before her, ten thousand times, to the objections of its adversaries. The contemplative Orders were founded for a special work in the Church, in order to pray, to love, and to expiate; like Mary, they sit continually at the feet of Our Lord, hearing His Word, and like her they have chosen the better part, and they have the divine promise that "it shall not be taken away from them."

A French writer says : " Passionate, loving desires to serve God are so pleasing to Him, that on three different occasions the inspired text calls Daniel a man of desires, *Vir desideriorum;* and if he is heard it is because, as the Angel Gabriel informs him, he is a man of desires, ' *Quia vir desideriorum es.*' Moses, disputing with the divine wrath, cries : ' Either forgive this people, or blot me out from the book of life '; and the Almighty allowed Himself to be vanquished. It is thus that conversions are, as it were, wrested from the hands of God. Holiness and prayer are the two great means of saving souls ; action and speech, necessary instruments as they are to santification, only come second. There is as much difference between a *doer* (if we may use the word) and an *apostle,* as between body and soul. How many humble women, unknown to this world, who having like Eustelle, prayed, wept, and sighed incessantly, whilst imploring the divine forgiveness for sinners, will at the last day see themselves surrounded by a multitude of the predestinate who will owe Heavon to their prayers, and be placed in the midst of the St. Vincent Ferrers, the St. Francis Xaviers, and the St. Dominics! Whereas, others, contrary perhaps to their expectations, and in spite of their labors, will not have one spiritual son to present to Our Lord, because these will have been *men of action*, without being saints and *men of prayer*."*

Clare's longing to save souls found an outlet in a very touching and natural way, in working for the good and sanctification of her own immediate belongings and home circle. Nothing can be more opposed to the spirit of true piety than that restless desire, so often shown by beginners in the paths of perfection, to accomplish great things abroad—whether in converting the heathen or educating the street Arab—whilst it neglects the means of doing good at its own doors. A special blessing seems to rest on those gentle ministrations, words, and acts of kindness which make virtue and piety attractive to those around us. And it was in these humble and unobtrusive duties that Clare was so great a proficient. If any of the servants were ill in the house, she was the first to go and visit them, and attend to their wants. Like all unselfish people (and the distinguishing feature of Clare's character was her great unselfishness), she was the foremost whenever there was any deed of kindness or charity to be performed. No headache, however violent, would stop her when the consolation or good of others was in question. Though Clare was by nature shy and retiring, so much so that a sudden word addressed to her would bring the blood

* Life of Marie Eustelle Harpain.

rushing to her cheek, this never stood in her way when she saw an opportunity of working for God or her neighbor. One of her favorite practices during the last year of her life in the world was to invite the servants into the schoolroom and speak to them of the love of God, and explain to them the lives of the saints.

Great as was Clare's longing to leave all to follow Christ in the way of life to which she felt herself called, it would be a great mistake to suppose that she did not suffer deeply when the time came to make the sacrifice of the fond ties which still bound her to earth. She was passionately attached to her father, and almost equally so to her brothers and sisters ; but she had ever ringing in her ears the words of Our Lord, "He that loveth father or mother more than Me is not worthy of Me ; and he that loveth son or daughter more than Me is not worthy of Me. And he that taketh not up his cross and followeth Me is not worthy of Me."

Whilst her future was still uncertain, she writes to her father as follows :

"I am longing to have a talk with you about myself and the Poor Clares. I long to be safe in my convent, *never* to come out of it—following the vocation God has, I hope and trust, called me to. ... The words of Our Lord, ' *You* have not chosen Me, but I have chosen you,' is a rather awful truth to contemplate. But I have prayed daily for so many years to know my vocation, that I quite trust I am not mistaken when I say I think that the Order of the Poor Clares is the one I believe God has called me to. ... I shall not be taken by surprise by the austerities, etc., as I go on purpose that all my senses, and every sort of power I possess, may be mortified and put down. It would be silly and absurd, indeed, to expect anything but that, so that with the strength of God's grace I hope to remain and die there."

The time had come, then, when Clare was to be allowed to carry all these longing desires of her heart, which already threatened to endanger her health and undermine her constitution, into effect. Her prayers were heard; her father withdrew his opposition, and the only question that remained to be settled was the particular Community she was to join. She had long known the Poor Clares at Bayswater, and to them her thoughts naturally turned. Whilst she was still uncertain, an accident drew her attention to a convent of the same Order abroad, the Community of the Poor Clares at Amiens. Two things attracted her towards this convent. In the first place, it enjoyed the immense privilege of Exposition of the Most Holy Sacrament, and in the second, it demanded of her a more than ordinary sacrifice. In this country, and in the neighborhood of London, she would have been secure of the occasional visits of her numerous family, her friends, and her relations, whereas, at Amiens she would be called on to put the sea between them and her, and the separation would therefore be more entire and complete. Accordingly, after all fitting inquiries had been made, and she had learnt, on competent authority, that the Community she proposed joining were living up to the primitive fervor of their rule, and were indeed noted for the holiness and asceticism of their lives, she asked and obtained leave to join the Order on the day previously mentioned by her in her letters, the Friday of Easter week, April 25th, 1861. This is a letter she wrote, on the Monday in Easter week, to an intimate friend and cousin:

"I was delighted to receive your letter the other day; many thanks for it. Is it not truly magnificent for me? I am really going to join the Poor Clares next Friday. I do not go to the convent at Bayswater, but to Amiens, as they have perpetual adoration joined to it. There is a Jesuit House at Amiens, and Uncle Richard wrote to one of the Fathers there to ask him about the convent. The account he gave was most satisfactory, though *agonizing* also. It is thoroughly according to the spirit of St. Clare, and a most fervent Community. The agonizing part is that the nuns say they have an immense number who go there to join them, and they are continually being sent away, on account of the great difficulty in following the rule. They have several novices now, but they do not expect that they will remain. They do not much like taking me, as they say the constitution can't be thoroughly formed at eighteen. However, God's will be done, for that *must* be mine. I could not sleep all night when I first heard I was going on Friday. I will indeed pray for you. I think God must love you in a very special manner, for He has sent you so many things to bear; and now the friend you love best He takes away from you. There was once a Heart so filled with sorrow that it had to give a loud cry. It was abandoned even by God Himself. 'My God, my God, why hast Thou forsaken me!' And all this was for love of you! and now He sends you something to suffer for love of Him. What a privilege the saints have always considered this! I often think that that great heart of yours, and all the capabilities He has endowed you with, must be meant to be spent in a different way from other mortals! Do pray for me, particularly on Friday ... Teresa * is very happy! I can't believe she is going to-morrow. It does seem so extraordinary. Our angel mother does indeed live among us as much and more than ever she did when on earth."

The next day she writes to N——. After repeating what she had said above, about her change of plans— that it was to Amiens, and not to Bayswater that she was bound,—she says:

"Pray a great deal for me, dearest N——, and thank our beloved Lord for such great love in choosing such an unworthy creature as myself to become a religious. I will *never* forget you, and will pray daily for you. Is it not wonderful about Teresa? I always thought it would be so. She enters this evening. And so this is to say farewell to you, dear N——, until we meet in that land where there are no more partings, but everlasting bliss and endless joy. I hope you have a great devotion to St. Joseph; he is, you know, the special patron of the interior life. I owe him a great deal, far more than I can ever say."

Once more she writes to this same dear friend, and as one reads it one feels that a cry of pain from this one who was to be left behind, who was to be without

* Her sister Teresa became a Sister of Charity at Westminster, where she died soon afterwards.

her for evermore, reached her, and perhaps for one instant ruffled the calm, or rather the blissful rapture, with which Clare contemplated parting with all—father, relations, friends, country, all things. It begins thus:

"Although it is midnight, I really cannot leave home without writing to you, and assuring you that you will ever be loved by me, and that you never *can* be forgotten. I was very glad indeed to receive your long letter this morning. But why do you think that I have changed in my feelings towards you? You must not think or say that, dearest N——, because it is so *untrue*. I am not worth all the love you bestow on me. You do not know me; if you did, you would not care for me as much as you do. But your letter was just like your own self, full of affection and generosity. You do me great kindness in praying for me. From my heart I thank you. . . . If I am allowed, I will certainly write to you; but I know they are very strict about letter writing, and one is very seldom allowed to write even to one's own home. Oh, N——, it seems too glorious, too magnificent to think that I shall actually one day be the spouse of Jesus! I will leave the life of our angel mother for your own private reading, but please give it to May, as it is hers. Farewell, then, dearest N——; increase daily in the love of the Blessed Sacrament. Let Jesus be all in all to you. *Be courageous*, and go always to the Sacred Heart in all your trials and afflictions. There is nothing so tender or so consoling as that adorable Heart. May you remain there for ever. I was so sorry I could not write to you by this day's post, but my time has been so occupied that I had no time to write you a long letter. The whole of this afternoon and evening I have been spending with Teresa at Westminster. But really now I *must* say farewell until we meet in that better land. May God bless you, and Mary, our sweet Mother, watch over you, and may the holy angels guard you and protect you, and may you never forget in your prayers your friend and cousin."

Then comes a very characteristic postscript:

"Don't you sympathize with me for preferring going to Amiens, far away, etc., etc."

One more letter Clare writes before starting for Amiens. This time it was to her uncle, Father Edmund Vaughan. She begins:

"It is a far greater trial for me than you have any idea of, not seeing you again before I leave for my home at Amiens. I fully intended coming to see you this week. I only knew on Good Friday I was going to Amiens to-day. Even then it was not thoroughly arranged, as I had heard nothing decided about the convent itself. It seems too glorious to think I am really going to-day! And yet it is true! How immensely loving of God to choose such a miserable creature as myself for His spouse! I will indeed pray every day for you, dearest uncle, and I will write to you when I am clothed, or before that, if it is possible. It is just time to start, so you will, I hope, excuse this blotty concern. A thousand thanks for your note, and for all your kindness and charity. Do remember me, *particularly* to-morrow. Do pray that I may persevere. The thought of my own unworthiness oppresses me so much at times, that if anything could make me come to a standstill, that would."

With these words Clare's life *in the world* closes. The next day saw her safely landed in that home so ardently longed for, which was to be hers for the short time that remained to her on earth. But this sketch, so imperfectly put together (from recollections, and from the letters she left behind), is now to be supplemented by a record of a thousand times greater interest to the spiritual-minded. It is that of Clare's inner life and practices of prayer during the nine months of her life as a Religious at Amiens till her death there in 1862. During these nine months her soul made marvellous strides in the paths of perfection, so as even to fill with astonishment the holy Community of which Clare considered herself the last and least worthy member. This life was drawn up by the confessor of the Community, the Rev. M. l'Abbé Herbet, from notes kept by the Religious, and was entitled " Notes on the Life and Death of Clare Vaughan, Sister Mary Clare of the Infant Jesus, who died in the odor of sanctity on the 20th of January, 1862."

CHAPTER VII.

Two or three verses borrowed from the fourth book of "The Following of Christ" will serve as an introduction to this little sketch that we have undertaken to give. In putting these words, which appear to sum up her life, into the mouth of our Poor Clare, we shall have furnished her with the means of exhibiting herself to us in her true character. This short passage will be the best explanation of the title which she loved to give herself, in the vividness of her faith and the ardor of her love, that of the Victim of the Most Holy Sacrament. "Lord, all things are Thine, that are in heaven and upon earth. I desire to offer myself up to Thee as a voluntary oblation, and to remain forever Thine. Lord, in the simplicity of my heart I offer myself to Thee this day, as Thy servant forevermore, for Thy homage, and for a sacrifice of perpetual praise. Receive me with this Sacred Oblation of Thy precious Body, which I offer to Thee this day in the invisible presence of assisting angels, that it may be for salvation unto me and all Thy people. Receive me with this Holy Oblation of Thy precious Body, which I offer Thee to-day, in the presence of Thy holy angels, invisible witnesses of Thy sacred mysteries, so that it may be a pledge of salvation to me and all the people."

These words, which a holy pen once inscribed, a life —amongst many others—has in our days devoted itself specially to illustrate. All that we have to say about this life, which, though short, was so full, is described in these words, "Receive me with the oblation of Thy precious Body." Yes, it was for the glory of the Holy Eucharist that this child was born, it was to this end that she lived—for this she died. If it is permitted to us to compare small things with great, we would even say that, as St. John received the mission to give testimony to the Word hidden beneath the veil of humanity, so this holy soul received the mission from Heaven to give testimony, in the narrow circle in which she moved, of that Light hidden under the veil of the most august Sacrament of the Altar. For her to live was to love and to adore. Death was, for her, to see and possess the all-loving God, who has deigned to assure us that "His delight is to be with the children of men."

Dedicated to God for years, indeed from her very birth, by the habits of her life and the desires of her heart, the time had now come when Clare was to become so in deed and in truth. It was not, however, without being well assured of the genuineness of her vocation that her father yielded at last to her pressing demand. On the 8th of April, 1861, he took her himself to Amiens, and handed her over to the Community of Poor Clares, Clare having chosen that house in preference to others on account of the Blessed Sacrament being perpetually exposed there, night and day, to the adoration of the faithful and the Religious of the Order. From our first interview (remarks the nun from whose notes this little work has been compiled), we drew Colonel Vaughan's attention to the fears which we all en-

ENTRANCE GATE TO THE MONASTERY AT AMIENS.

tertained, that his daughter, on account of her delicacy of constitution, and her bringing up, would never be able to accustom herself to our way of life; but he assured us that the longing desire of his daughter to consecrate herself to God was killing her by inches, and that he thought that the effect of the observance of our Rule on her health, austere though it be, was less to be dreaded than an opposition to her wishes, which threatened to undermine it altogether. We gave into this reasoning, knowing as we did by experience that calmness of mind and contentment of heart very often exercise a wonderfully salutary influence, even on constitutions already threatened with disease. Clare was accordingly presented to the Community, which was assembled in Chapter for that purpose. The renown of her virtues, her eminent piety and angelic innocence, had already preceded her amongst us. His Eminence Cardinal Wiseman, had spoken in these terms of her in a letter addressed to us with regard to this occasion:

"I confide a beloved lamb of my flock, Clare Vaughan, to your care, so that she may associate herself with you in your mortifications and your prayers, some of which I trust will be for us. You will become possessed of an exquisite flower, a flower of innocence and virtue, which I regret deeply parting with; she is one of those souls which Our Lord has been pleased to preserve in their baptismal purity."

This high praise, coming with the weight of such great and venerable authority, increased the desire we had previously felt to possess so holy a soul in the midst of us. Still, our first desire was to know and accomplish the holy will of God with regard to her admission. Thus to make sure of the truth of her vocation, we addressed the usual questions to her, not allowing her for a moment to remain ignorant of the trying and penitential side of the new form of life which she proposed adopting. We asked her, amongst other things, how, having never done any manual labor, she would care to descend to the common and menial tasks in which the every-day life of a religious community consists; such as sweep the house, wash the plates and dishes, prepare the food, etc.; but to all these questions, and others similar, her invariable answer was, "I will try to do it as soon as you have shown me the way," thus putting aside one difficulty for another, hers being, not about doing these things, but doing them well. But another obstacle, this time an almost insurmountable one to any courage but Clare's, presented itself. In her father's house Clare, on account of her extreme weakness of digestion, had always eaten meat on days of abstinence; on the other hand, the Rule of the Order of Poor Clares enjoins perpetual abstinence from meat, and this rule is so absolute that dispensation is not even given in cases of serious illness. The pious postulant's answer to this objection was that once she was admitted she would do like the rest, and partake cheerfully of all that was put before her; and in order to persuade her interrogators to share her own feelings of confidence, she ingenuously assured them that her stomach would follow the lead of her head, and that both would yield obedience to our holy Rule: "for," said she, "though the slightest study or application of the mind gives me violent pains, I never feel any when I pray; then the time always appears too short." No argument having any effect in shaking her determination to become a Poor Clare, the Community proceeded to confer upon her admission into the house, and she was accordingly, as is the custom in those cases, re-conducted into the outer enclosure while the deliberation went on.

"You will pray hard that the will of God may be made known," said one of the Sisters who accompanied her. "Oh, yes," she cried very earnestly, "I have already prayed with all my heart for this intention." "But," added the Sister, "when the moment comes for you to make the sacrifice for good and all, and you have to take leave of your father, your courage may ooze out, and you may not be able to make up your mind to let him return all alone to England." At these words the poor child gave utterance to a most decided "No!" which revealed the fervor of a will triumphing over all the instincts of nature at bidding of faith. Tears, caused more by the fear of being rejected than by the thought of being separated from him whom she loved best on earth, flowed down her cheeks. One could only console her and tell her to confide in God, who will never allow those who trust in Him to be confounded. And thus, in spite of the natural fears entertained for her health with such a change of life and habits in prospect, the Chapter judged that it was the Divine Will that this young postulant should be admitted, at least on probation, even though it should be at the risk of returning her to her family if the trial was beyond her strength. But Our Lord had particular designs on this soul, and He willed their accomplishment for His honor and glory. Clare was accordingly received into the Community. It would be well-nigh impossible for us, the Superior of the Convent declared, to describe the joy she showed when the good news was announced to her, and even more difficult to put into words her happiness when she was admitted into the Community. It was even greater when she saw herself stripped of her worldly dress in order to be invested with the poor and humble habit of religion. The Prophet asks this question, " Will a virgin forget her ornaments, or a bride her stomacher?"* Truly may we answer this question in the affirmative. This wonder is daily accomplished, and the House of St. Clare at Amiens showed it for the hundredth time renewed. In truth no words can say how beautiful, how attractive is this most loving Spouse, who offers Himself to the soul of man in order that He may possess it alone. Thus with what fervor of gratitude the new betrothed of Our Lord gave to each one of the Sisters the customary kiss of peace, with what fervor of joy she thanked them for the favor they had granted her!

These preliminaries gone through, she was confided to the care of the Mistress of Novices, from whom, it is unnecessary to say, she received the most cordial welcome. But if the Noviceship congratulated itself on this addition to its number, not less the whole Community was soon to appreciate and recognize the value of the precious treasure with which Our Lord had en-

* Jeremias ii. 32.

riched it. Sister Mary Clare of the Infant Jesus (the name she chose in religion) was indeed, as Cardinal Wiseman expressed it, an angel of innocence and sweetness. Her countenance was stamped with such a gentle expression of candor, her manner partook of so much grace and dignity, everything about her, in fine, betrayed something so absolutely angelic, that one might already have taken her for an inhabitant of Heaven. Her very presence shed joy and peace on those who approached her; one felt one's self naturally drawn to her, and it was impossible to see her without loving her.

Soon after she was received into the convent at Amiens, she writes to her sister, the Visitation nun, in the following terms:

"DEAREST GLADYS:—I have just been sweeping! I am dreadfully afraid that the dust, which is so good for one's health, they say, should make me live forever! I can't tell you how happy I am here. I should not have thought it was possible to be so happy, and yet to have so many trials and crosses. To be a daughter of St. Clare and a true spouse of Christ one must be dead to one's self; but how true it is that Our Lord puts unspeakable joys in the Cross! Who can describe the joy the soul feels in suffering for the love of Him who loved us even to the 'folly of the Cross!' Pray for me, I beg of you, dearest Gladys, that I may correspond to the grace of my sublime vocation. What courage and generosity it requires! I beg of you to implore those virtues for me of our Beloved Lord. I am simply longing for the day of my profession, but, poor wretch that I am, I have not yet been clothed! I am hoping to be clothed in the month of September. We have two Masses here every day, and the Blessed Sacrament always exposed night and day. It is indeed Heaven before its time. On the Feast of our seraphic mother, St. Clare, every one asks a favor of Mother Abbess. I am going to ask her to give me the name of Sister Mary Magdalen, victim of the Blessed Sacrament.

"I don't think anything will ever be able to drag me from here,—I am always dreading they will send me away. Yesterday, when I was going to the cellar to draw the beer, I found a little hole to hide myself in. I would infinitely prefer spending my life there than be sent away from this place, where Jesus Christ is so loved. I am resolved never to leave this spot. If they want to turn me out of doors, I shall begin to pray that something may go wrong with the lock! There is a very large Community here: there are thirty-four professed nuns, without counting the novices. I cannot tell you how good they all are to me. This convent is entirely according to the spirit of the seraphic Founder. We almost live in the presence of the Blessed Sacrament. Three hours of the day are spent in household work, as there are no lay-sisters here. *All* the nuns have but one desire in life, and that is to belong to the number of the 'beloved poor' of Jesus Christ. We get up at half-past eleven for Matins, which lasts till three o'clock; then we go to bed again till half-past five. It does not take us long to dress. I cannot tell you, darling, how glad I was to see you on my way here. It was you exactly; you are not the least bit changed,

—only your voice, which is now more like the Rolls's. Before I got here I wrote from the hotel to tell them at home all about you. It is very agonizing to think that as long as we live we shall never see each other again! How scattered all the members of the family are! But what joy and happiness to think we shall all meet again together in Heaven, all virgins 'following the Lamb whithersoever He goeth!' And after all, *what is life?* It is so short—though sometimes it seems long to the exiled. Will you tell Reverend Mother that I thank her so much for all her kindness to me, and that I shall never forget her kind hospitality, and that I hope she will not forget to pray for me? Will you show dear Madame de la Pasture this letter, as I have no time to write to her? Give her my love. I have not forgotten Charles's delightful prophecy about me,—that I shall stay here till I die!"

The new postulant, from the very first, had to submit to the hardest trial which could have been imposed upon her—that of not being allowed to observe the Rule in all its integrity. This measure of precaution was wise and prudent, and notwithstanding her repugnance at being exempted, and her entreaties that she might not be spared, she had to submit and place her merit in her obedience rather than in her acts of mortification. Apart from this suffering which, though a very real one, her common sense and, above all, her religious feeling quickly enabled her to conquer, she took infinite pleasure in the company of her Sisters, and lost no occasion of showing them how happy she was to find herself in their midst. Taking the intensest pleasure in all the religious exercises in which she was allowed to join, she carried the greatest fervor into all the practices of her new state of life. The only cloud which occasionally troubled the peace of her happy and peaceful existence, was the fear lest her health should be found an insurmountable obstacle to her definite admission into the house. One day she heard some of the Sisters saying to each other, that novices could not, in conscience, be admitted into the Community who were not able to keep the Rule. She took these words as intended for herself, and it was with the greatest difficulty that she was consoled. "I would much rather," she said, in her expressive and energetic style, "that my legs and arms were cut off, than that I was refused admission. No," added she, "nothing will ever be able to tear me from here."

A letter which she wrote soon after her arrival at Amiens, to her uncle and director, Father Vaughan, has been preserved, and shows how deeply she entered, heart and soul, into the duties of her new life.

"It was a real pleasure to me to receive your letter a few days ago; I was just thinking of asking permission to write to you when I received your letter. Many thanks for it. It always does me good to hear from you. I am very happy here in this true home of St. Clare. I have found all I wanted. The Blessed Sacrament perpetually exposed night and day is all my consolation and joy. What a comfort to think you pray for me! A true Poor Clare must live on Calvary, must wear a crown of thorns, and by her three vows must nail herself to the Cross of her crucified Spouse if she wishes to reach her home in Heaven. *I, too,* am dreadfully tempted to be jealous of dearest Teresa's happiness! Was it not a beautiful death to die immediately after making her vows? She has heard now those glorious words, *Veni, Sponsa Christi! Accipe coronam tuam quam tibi Dominus preparavit in æternam.* Oh, how swiftly our dear Lord prepared her soul to follow among the other virgins in Heaven! I heard she was immensely changed the three weeks before her death, and her only delight was to talk on spiritual subjects. She used often to say, laughing, to me: 'Oh, Uncle Edmund never understands me, and I can't get on with him; I wish I could send him my soul without my body. It is only that he cares for!' We live entirely in the Church. I have such a beautiful place there, quite, *quite* close to our dear Lord. It is so magnificent rising in the night to sing His praises! and then our adoration directly after Matins. I am never tired—on the contrary, it is when I do *not* go to Matins that I am tired. I wash and clean the dishes and saucepans, etc., dust and sweep the corridors and stairs, etc. We have no lay-Sisters. Here holy poverty is loved passionately. I have never seen Religious so completely devoted to God as they are here. Our Reverend Mother Abbess is perfect in humility and patience. Two or three days ago, in the refectory, she knelt down before each of the Religious and kissed their feet. She did the same also to the novices. I am so immensely grateful to you for your prayers! Pray for me, that I may accept generously the crosses and trials our beloved Lord sends me. The life of a Poor Clare *must* be a life of suffering. We go to Holy Communion most wonderfully often; even the novices go four or five times in the week. The professed go every day. Last week I went every day. We have two Masses and Benediction every day. We have a *perfect* Mistress of Novices. Oh, pray for me that I may not abuse such incomprehensible graces and favors! I feel so dreadfully frightened about my perseverance, and that I shall be sent away, for I feel so thoroughly that it would be simply what I deserve. However, I told our Mother Mistress, the other day, that I have found a place in the convent where I intend hiding myself if they do send me away, and she gave me her permission that there I should make my profession. I am in the hopes that I shall have the name of ' Sœur Madeleine, Victime du Saint Sacrement.' Many of the Sisters call me by that name already. Others call me the *Sponsa Christi*. I find great difficulty in taking the vegetable diet here. At times, even, I can't swallow at all, even the bread. But the nuns are so full of kindness and charity! they are always making Novenas for me, so I have already conquered many difficulties. I hope to begin to fast the end of this month. According to our Rule we are obliged to fast for a month before we take the habit. I read the Constitutions every day in the refectory. The diet is very strict here—only one meal at twelve, nothing at all before that time, and at six o'clock a piece of bread and some beer. There is nothing for which I have more devotion than praying for sinners. I love them with my utmost heart; nearly all my prayers are for them!—divine office I say for them, and I will unite them in future with the labors of the Redemptorists. There is nothing on earth so sad to think of as that souls should be lost whom Our Lord's love *could not help* creating, in spite of all the sins He saw they would commit against Him. Our Reverend Mother Abbess has a burning love for sinners. Her soul is like a temple dedicated to Heaven—like the Pantheon in Rome, lighted only from above. All the Religious here are in a Confraternity for the conversion of England, and England has a share of all their prayers and penance. The whole life of a Poor Clare is a life of reparation. Now, dearest uncle, I have a favor to ask you. I want to make a compact with you ; I will offer up Holy Communion for you every Thursday if you will do something *generous* in that way for me. Please do not forget to answer this. I am delighted to hear about Kenelm. I hope he will be a Redemptorist ; I pray for that. I am now going to attend Chapter. Our Mother Abbess and our Mistress of Novices present you their respects, and the latter says she will be delighted when you write to me, as your letters can do nothing but good ; and the Community will be too happy to pray for your missions when you write about them. I must now conclude this immensely long letter. I don't believe you will have time or the immense patience to read it all. But what I do beg is that you entreat, when you are at the altar, that I may be a spouse of Our Blessed Lord's when He comes to take all His to the eternal Marriage-feast. There are forty Religious here, but there is not one English nun amongst them. Pray for me."

Five months elapsed, and Clare was still a postulant; and her superiors, though not wanting in encouragement, had not as yet dropped one word—such as in ordinary cases, when no reason exists for deferring the clothing, would have been said—to lead her to suppose that she was shortly to be admitted to that ceremony. Her courage, however, never failed, and she had stood fairly well the hardships of fasting and the other austerities of the Rule, which for some little time she had followed in all their strictness. Prudence was on the side of a longer trial, and its counsels prevailed; but how was it possible to resist such fervent desires, such ardent appeals? A month more was passed in uncertainty when, vanquished by such persistent fidelity, the Religious, having taken the advice of the venerable ecclesiastical authority under whose care their house is placed, consented to receive the pious postulant into the number of their novices. Our Divine Saviour, who takes pleasure in doing the will of those who love Him, deigned to hear and grant the longing wishes of this dear child; and as the thoughts and wills of all men are in His hands, He so ordered it that the whole Community was found unanimously to declare in her favor. A letter she writes to her brother, the Rev. Kenelm Vaughan, dates from about this time:

"I was indeed delighted to receive your letter some time ago. I can easily imagine that you have to suffer, but, as you say, 'When a soul is resolved to suffer for God, the pain of suffering ceases.' Many thanks for the books you sent me. I like St. Gertrude's very much. I have not read yet Dalgairn's work. French books are the most acceptable here, as the nuns, being all French (except one), cannot understand a word of English, and they are glad of a new French work or French prayerbook. I am writing to tell you some glorious news. I am to take the holy habit of St. Clare on the Feast of St. Teresa. . . . I hope you will offer up Holy Communion for me on that great day, that I may take up my cross valiantly and follow my Spouse to death. Yesterday, being the Feast of our Father, St. Francis, we had an hour's recreation. We have recreation four times a year. I pray a great deal for you. Every day I meet our angel mother and dear Teresa and the entire family in the Sacred Heart before the Blessed Sacrament. We shall never meet in any other home but that, until we arrive at our eternal home in Heaven. How is Uncle Edmund? I often think Our Lord chooses the Poor Clares to honor His suffering life, and the Redemptorists to honor His active life. I hope Mary gets on with———. However, God will have her soon—as soon as she is *fledged*.* Birds fledged must fly, and ours fly all in one direction—*like the dove, to be at rest.*†

SR. CLARE TO MISS BELLASIS, RELIGIOUS OF THE H. C. J.

COUVENT DES PAUVRES CLARISSES,
Amiens, October, 1861.

MY DEAREST MARY:—

" I was delighted to receive your letter to-day, and to hear that you are going to be clothed next Friday. I congratulate you upon such happiness with all my heart;

* Clare's sister Mary died in 1884, when prioress of St. Augustine's Priory, Newton Abbot.

† Of her eight brothers, six became priests, while all her sisters entered convents.

and now you will congratulate me when I tell you that I, too, am going to receive the holy habit of our seraphic mother, St. Clare, next Tuesday, the Feast of St. Teresa. I enter into retreat to-morrow, and will indeed pray much for you. Do not forget me on my clothing day. I am so grateful to you, dear Mary, for having prayed so much for me.

"I am immensely happy here. Oh, how we ought to thank God unceasingly for such wondrous love and mercy in choosing us, and above all, in choosing me to be His spouse! Those were beautiful words you copied for me, of St. Francis of Sales. Indeed, we must never forget that it is Jesus with His cross that we espouse, and that '*une vie sans croix, est une vie sans amour.*'

"But I am talking very bravely, when my actions, alas! speak so differently. It is impossible to be more cowardly and more full of self-love than I am. However, I am hoping all things from my retreat. Pray that I may not care what happens, or what I have to suffer from my own nature, etc., so I only become like our seraphic mother, St. Clare.

"I am delighted that you have such devotion to our Father, St. Francis, and shall indeed say a prayer for your dear mistress, who has inspired you all with such a devotion.

"What a comfort that your mamma is reconciled to your being a nun, and that your health is so much better! Mine also is infinitely better. I am able to fast every day, and go to Matins, etc.

"Farewell, dearest Mary. Is it not strange that my clothing happens to fall on my beloved sister's feast?

Pray also to her for me, as I will for you. My kindest love to Mary Teresa. Ask her to pray for me.

"Believe me, dearest Mary, in the Sacred Heart of Jesus,

"Your Very Affectionate Sister,

"CLARE VAUGHAN.

"I do not know what name I shall have. Excuse this hurried line."

MY DEAREST MARY:—

"It is impossible to tell you how grateful I feel to you for your kindness in sending me such a beautiful account of the death of my beloved Teresa. It has been a very heavy affliction to me, but it is selfish to grieve when I know she is happy; and the far more my companion now than she was ever in days past. She was too pure and holy for this sinful earth, and she has gone to the home of her love, to join our angel mother and those bright bands of virgins who follow the Lamb wheresoever He goeth.

"Oh no! I feel myself, she will not have to grieve over her intense bliss. What a glorious death, to die immediately after becoming the spouse of the Lamb!

"I am delighted to hear you go to St. Leonard's on the 21st. I will pray to my darling Teresa for you. She is always by my side now. Pray for me, that I may have some courage put into my cowardly nature. Your letter was read aloud (translated) to all the novices yesterday. Ma Mere Maitresse talks of having it read aloud in the refectory after it is translated.

"Kindest love to Rothe. If you see Miss Pole, will you

beg her to write and tell me all the last words of my most beloved sister?"

The 15th of October, the Feast of St. Teresa, was fixed upon for the clothing ceremony. Although the lives of the daughters of St. Francis may be said to be spent in a perpetual retreat, yet to prepare the future novice for her mystical espousals, eight days of even more absolute solitude are enjoined by the Rule. If in these days of retreat her fervor increased, her love became still more ardent, and her life-long desire to die in order to be united with her Lord and her only Love became more ardent than before, it may be also said that God, on the other hand, filled her soul with even more abundant graces, and with His most consoling and choicest benedictions.

He would not as yet break asunder the ties which attached her to the earth, but He purified and detached her heart more and more; the sword of sacrifice remained suspended over her head, but the victim was preparing, and already from the summits of Thabor she could catch sight of her Calvary.

Those who were witnesses of her clothing still preserve a recollection of that day.

"I think I see her again," the Vicar-General lately said to us (talking of this touching ceremony, at which he had presided), "standing with her pale countenance slightly tinged with that bright light with which we paint the Seraphim on fire with divine love; dressed in a simple garment coming down to her feet, which were naked, according to the custom of the Order, her hair loose and falling in thick masses on her shoulders,

INTERIOR OF CHAPEL WHERE CLARE RECEIVED THE HOLY HABIT.

her head crowned with thorns, and holding a crucifix in her hands. When she appeared in the middle of the choir we were reminded of one of the virgins of the early Church being led to the spot of her martyrdom; or, to borrow an even higher resemblance, we thought of the Angel of the Resurrection, seated on the stone of the sepulchre, and saying to the holy women, 'He is not here. Behold the place where they laid Him.'" *

Once clad in the liveries of Jesus Christ by her nun's habit, Sister Mary Clare of the Infant Jesus proceeded rapidly to strip off all that remained in her of the old man and to put on the new, who, as St. Paul says, was created to sanctity and truth. The great means of effecting this transfiguration, or rather substitution of the Creator for the creature, is in the devout and continual frequentation of that august Sacrament, after whose reception the soul of man may indeed cry, "It is no longer I who live, but Jesus Christ who lives in me!" We have already drawn attention to the fact that the distinctive characteristic of the Sister Mary Clare—her particular attraction, her vocation in life—seemed to be to honor Jesus, present and hidden beneath the Eucharistic veil; it was to follow out this call that she had resisted the efforts made by Cardinal Wiseman to persuade her to remain in London, as well the wishes of her uncle, the Bishop of Plymouth, who would gladly have welcomed her into one of the religious communities established in his diocese. Seeing, therefore, that all Clare's longing desires were realized

* Mark xvi. 6.

by her admission into the convent of Poor Clares, which enjoys the happy privilege of Perpetual Adoration, it is not astonishing that she should have given herself up utterly to a practice which formed the happiness of her life. As the magnet turns to the North Pole, so did all her thoughts, desires, affections, turn to the spot where Jesus resided. Even when sleeping at night she loved to lie with her face turned towards Him who was the desire of her heart, saying to Him, no doubt, as the Spouse of the Canticle, "I sleep, but my heart watches." She would often, when passing outside the chapel, prostrate in adoration before Our Lord, and kiss in devout affection the door which led into His Presence. In her eager desire to add to the number of her visits to the Blessed Sacrament, she used to contrive to leave a book, or something, in the chapel, which would give her an excuse for a few moments of adoration of Our Lord. She used often to implore permission to spend the entire night in the presence of the Blessed Sacrament, ingenuously urging "that it was impossible to sleep when one knew He was there." In the early days after her arrival at the convent, it had been considered advisable not to put her name down among the night watchers; but as soon as she found out what had been done, she was quite inconsolable, and some compensation in other ways had to be made to her before she could be persuaded to dry her tears.

The time spent in the sanctuary was always too short for her, and she was often heard to say, when the hour of adoration was over, "What! is it really time to go? But we have only just begun!" St. Augustine wrote in one of his works, "Give me a heart which truly loves, and it will understand my meaning."* We also must require from a heart that it should love, in order that it should understand what we have got to say. One day when the bell had rung for the Community to go to bed, and all, with the exception of those who were watching before the Blessed Sacrament, were resting for the night, the pious victim of the Blessed Sacrament having satisfied the obligation of obedience to the Rule by retiring to her cell with the others, finding nothing so sweet as to watch near her Beloved, got up from the camp bedstead where she had thrown herself down, all dressed, and taking the quilt which served for her to rest her head upon when she was worn out, spent the remainder of the night in the cloister adjoining the church. The nuns on coming out from Matins, or from watching before the Blessed Sacrament, were astonished to find her stretched on the bare boards of the cloister, having succumbed to sleep, which, for once, had triumphed over her resolution.

This ardent love of hers for the Blessed Sacrament showed itself everywhere, and in all things; in the smallest, as in the greatest. For instance, if it was a question of sweeping the stalls in the choir, in that part of the church which is reserved for the nuns, she

* "Give me a lover, and he will understand what I say. Give me a man of desires, one who hungers. Give me in this desert a pilgrim who is athirst. Give me one who is sighing after the eternal fountain —he will understand what I say. But if my words fall on cold ears they will have no sense."—St. Augustine *in Johan.*, tract XXV.— Translated by M. Allies.

found in this common and ordinary occupation, because by its means she was able to pass backwards and forwards before the little opening from whence one could see the Sacred Host, an excuse for satisfying her love and devotion. As soon as she reached this spot, her work made no further progress; she could not tear herself away from It; whilst her hands mechanically dusted the step and supports on each side of the grille, her eyes and heart were fixed on the monstrance which held the object of all her love. When the Blessed Sacrament was exposed in the inner grille, for the benefit of the Community, it was a great consolation to this holy novice to place herself in the middle of the choir, so as to get nearer the Sacred Host and obtain a better view of It; there she remained motionless, and, as it were, rapt in an ecstasy of love. When, however, to avoid singularity it was thought better to forbid her this outward manifestation of her ardent love, at the word of her Superior she submitted humbly; but the sacrifice was one of which God alone knows all the value.

What we are now going to relate may appear very insignificant to some who only care for what appears great in the eyes of the world; but for those souls of whom Our Lord spoke when He said, "I give Thee thanks, O Father, Lord of Heaven and earth! because Thou hast hidden these things from the wise and the prudent, and hast revealed them to little ones"*—to these souls these little details will not be without a certain interest and attraction. Let us, then, allow the

* St. Luke x. 21.

Sister, from whose narrative these details are drawn, to give us her account of it.

"We are in the habit, as is customary in all cases when the Blessed Sacrament is exposed, of placing several lighted candles on each side of the monstrance where the Blessed Sacrament is placed. Thus when, during the night, one of the candles had nearly burned down, or had gone out, knowing the happiness it was to our dear Sister of the Infant Jesus to approach Our Lord, we handed over to her the care of replacing them without appearing to attach much importance to the duty. Never shall we forget the profound respect and reverence with which she acquitted herself of this office, which to her was such an enviable privilege. Before she left the spot she would respectfully and lovingly kiss the bars which separate our choir from the sanctuary, where the Blessed Sacrament was exposed, and when doing so she reminded us of that beautiful passage in the fourth book of 'The Following of Christ:' 'For who, humbly approaching to the fountain of sweetness, doth not carry thence some little sweetness? Or who, standing by a copious fire, doth not derive therefrom some little heat? And Thou art a fountain ever full and overflowing. Thou art a fire always burning and never failing. Wherefore, if I may not draw out of the fulness of the fountain, nor drink to satiety, I will at least set my mouth to the opening of this heavenly pipe, that so I may draw thence some little drops to allay my thirst, and may not wholly wither away.'*

* "Following of Christ," fourth book, c. iv.

"It would almost seem superfluous, after all we have said with regard to the ardent love of our holy novice for the Sacrament of the Altar, to speak of the fervor of her Communions, and of the profound self-abasement with which she assisted every day at the Holy Sacrifice of the Mass. It was, above all, at Mass that she united herself with Jesus our Victim, and offered herself with Him for the salvation of sinners. This spirit of reparation was, it may be said, the distinctive character of the tender piety of Sister Mary Clare of the Infant Jesus. To expiate the outrages which Our Lord receives in the Sacrament of the Altar, and to obtain the conversion of poor sinners, was the object of all her desires. Her prayers and her intentions were all directed to this sublime end, and thus she had a special devotion to the Litany of Reparation which is recited every evening by the daughters of St. Francis in the Community at Amiens. Hardly had the first words been pronounced than her head was turned towards the tabernacle, and with clasped hands and eyes fixed on the Sacred Host, she answered every invocation with the greatest fervor. This exercise of reparation was so dear to her, and took such a prominent place in her thoughts, that even in her sleep, or when she was not fully conscious of what she was doing, she used sometimes to put her cord round her neck as if to pray, and then, when entirely awake, she would repeat with every breath she drew, 'O my God, Thou art not loved!—Thou art so constantly offended!' Then sometimes she would draw deep sighs, and after a few minutes' silence would continue, 'My God! behold me;

Thou hast given me a body; I offer it once more to Thee; strike it—strike me, but spare poor sinners.' And then she would give herself a severe discipline. 'I consent,' she said, another time, 'to remain on earth till the end of the world, if by that means I could save one single soul.' On another occasion she was heard to cry, 'O my God, where is Thy divine justice? Thou hast given it up; there is no sign of anything but Thy mercy on earth; and yet sinners continue to offend Thee! No, beloved Lord, Thou art not loved. But I love Thee, or at least I desire to love Thee!'

"Then she would repeat the *Parce Domine*. At the hour when this angelic soul was earning for herself and for sinners that satisfaction which is exacted in order to complete the price of the ransom offered by the Redeemer of mankind—according to that wonderful word of St. Paul, who says, 'I fill up those things that are wanting of the sufferings of Christ'*—at that same hour of the silent, solitary night, a young girl of the world, a victim—uncrowned—of its laws and exigencies, is returning home, worn out with fatigue and excitement. As her carriage glides past the wall of the convent she hears the bell calling its voluntary recluses to prayer, and perhaps she says to herself, 'What is the use of nuns?' I will tell you; it is *to expiate*. After this night of enjoyment which you have spent at a ball or a theatre, another night will come—a night of agony and extremity of suffering. You will then lie on your bed, face to face with eternity, which you must encounter alone, and without assistance. You do not dare,

* Colossians i. 24.

or perhaps cannot pray; but some one has prayed for you; and doing violence to Heaven has obtained what you were not worthy of hoping for. That is the use of nuns. At this moment there is only question of the word of Our Lord, 'Amen, amen, I say to you, that you shall lament and weep, but the world will rejoice; but I will see you again, and your heart shall rejoice, and your joy no man shall take from you.'* Each has his portion. On the one hand, tears; but tears which are not without sweetness; on the other, pleasures; but pleasures which are not without bitterness, and which but too often are precursors of eternal woe.

"Sister Mary Clare had been offered her choice, and her choice had not caused her much hesitation. Like Jesus Christ, who had been offered joys and had preferred the Cross, she desired no other heritage, and, strange to say, she found this portion the most precious, this chalice the most inebriating; and so in accepting the sacrifice asked of her she had, even for her happiness in this world, chosen 'the better part.' Let us listen to the holy transports—we were almost going to say the delirious accents—which sometimes escaped from her heart and were poured from her lips. In reading them one would almost think one had come on a page from the life of St. Mary Magdalene of Pazzi, that great saint who, transported with divine love, used to go and ring the convent bell in the middle of the night in order to invite all men to come and do homage to her Divine Spouse. 'O Love, my beloved Love!' Sister Mary Clare would exclaim, 'how happy I am to be

* John xvi. 20, 22.

here! Everything breathes of the love of Thee; everything speaks to me of Thy love. What intense happiness it is to me to think of it! When I meet a nun, I say to myself, O Love, it is Thou who hath called her! and thus with all the Sisters. I can never help repeating, O Love, since it is Thy love, and Thine alone, which hath called her to be Thy spouse! O Jesus, my God, how I love thee! I love Thee enormously; I love Thee alone, and shall die of love unless Thou lovest me.'

"Strange to relate, it was in French that our Sister expressed herself so fluently on these occasions, God permitting it, no doubt, for the greater edification of the Community; for being but imperfectly acquainted with our language, she preferred in her ordinary exercises of devotion and prayers to make use of the English language. At times, such as we are alluding to, she was so utterly absorbed in God that she was insensible to everything. Nothing she heard or saw made any impression upon her; the most deafening noise going on around her, her name being called, and the efforts made to get her out of this state had no effect upon her. But at the word of the Mother Abbess, or if the Mistress of Novices addressed her, in the name of obedience she recovered at once the use of her senses, and could join the rest of the Religious in going to the choir.

"Once she happened to find herself alone with one of her Sister novices at the half-hour's adoration during the day-time; they fastened the door to prevent being taken by surprise, and, with ropes around their necks, prostrated in the middle of the choir, recited in this position the prayers of reparation. The young Sister who was with her did not dare to remain long in this position for fear of being seen, but Sister Mary Clare lay there without moving, till her companion, hearing a slight noise outside, ran to her to tell her of it. It was not without much difficulty that she could rouse her from the profound abstraction into which she was plunged."

Nothing, however, could better reveal the interior dispositions of immolation of this soul, whose one instinct was reparation, than an heroic project which she formed in company with another Sister, from whose lips we derive the story.

Very near the spot occupied by Sister Mary Clare in choir, a picture is hung representing one of the most touching scenes of the Passion of Our Lord, the Scourging at the Pillar. The eyes of the novice therefore were continually being drawn towards this picture, and neither they, nor her heart, could detach themselves from it. This, then, was what occurred to her.

But before telling our readers, we feel we must prepare their minds a little for what follows, lest perhaps some might find exaggeration or improbability in the story.

Perhaps there is no one who has not once in the course of their lives felt, when confronted with some danger, real or imaginary, what is called the sensation of vertigo. Those who have traversed the mountain passes of the Alps or Pyrenees, on the edge of abysses, which would appear practicable only to the foot of the wild goat, know what this sensation is like. Vertigo is a sort of oscillation of a natural instinct which balances between two opposing forces, one of which attracts and the other repels. Sister Mary Clare had sounded the profound abysses of the humiliations and sorrows of the Man-God, and a pious vertigo, similar to the holy folly spoken of by the great apostle, had taken possession of her. Nature, on the one hand, revolted from the terrible spectacle, and grace on the other was, as it were, fascinated and carried away by it. Let us see what she proposes to one of her Sisters, who listens to her with an admiration not unmingled with awe:

" Do you wish to love Our Lord? " she asked. " Undoubtedly," was the answer.

" Then listen," said she, " listen. We will go and try to find a big cord, as well as the crown of thorns which is in the noviceship; then we will ask leave to remain alone to-night to watch before the Blessed Sacrament. After Matins (if we get leave), when all the nuns have gone to bed, we will shut ourselves in, and you will fasten me to the bars of the grille with the rope which I shall fasten round my neck; then I shall put on the crown of thorns; Our Lord will forgive us for extinguishing for a few moments the sanctuary lamp; then you will provide yourself with a discipline, and will use it with all your strength, so that I shall be all bleeding; then we will prostrate and offer ourselves as victims of reparation to Jesus in the Holy Sacrament. ' Behold us!' we shall say, ' O Lord, it is for love of Thee, to make reparation to Thee, to obtain salvation for sinners, that we are in this state'; then we will recite eight times for this intention the Litanies of Reparation, and fifty times the *Parce Domine.*"

This, then, was the scheme formed by her who was called, and signed herself in her letters, the Victim of the Blessed Sacrament. If it was not put into execution, it was only because the Mother Abbess would not give permission for anyone to remain in chapel after the rest of the Religious left it.

With what offences, then, had this mortified soul, who was ever so hard on herself, to reproach her conscience with? Was it with the guilt of sin? She had preserved her baptismal innocence unstained. The pleasures of the world, in which she had mixed but rarely, had not even thrown a shadow upon the delicacy of her conscience: and since she had sought the shade of the cloister, this lily of purity, protected evermore in the closed garden of the Spouse, had but grown each day in grace and beauty. The faults of which she accused herself with such anguish were but the slight faults into which nature is liable to be surprised—passing distractions, a forgetfulness, more or less involuntary, of some prescription of the Rule. And with this virtue of innocence she united that of love of suffering. It would seem as if God intended to give in to the desires, as one might say, of her life, that in its due measure it resembled that of her Saviour in being one long cross and martyrdom. She suffered almost continually from headaches which caused her the acutest suffering. The violent pains which she endured in other parts of her body obliged her sometimes to lie down on the ground, but no pains that she was called upon to endure made her look upon suffering otherwise than as a dearly loved friend and sister. Her one desire was to be on the Cross with Jesus.

"Believe me," she wrote on one occasion, "the most admirable science is to know how to suffer; the greatest cleverness is to know how to suffer well; and, in fine, the happiest fate is never to be a single moment without suffering." "A life without crosses," she wrote again, "is a life without love. ... We shall have an eternity for enjoyment, but only in this life can we suffer."

It is easy to understand that with these dispositions no complaint ever found its way to her lips. Who does not know the solace and consolation it is, in the midst of one's sufferings, to confide one's troubles to one's friends and those who come to visit us? It would appear as if pain partly borne by compassion was lighter and less overwhelming. Sister Mary Clare, however, was exempt from this weakness. To see her, calm and recollected, one would think it was some one else who was suffering. If she was questioned about her health, her answers, though ever truthful, were short and to the point.

The day she entered the noviceship, she said to one of the Religious, with a great air of satisfaction, "Everyone here is very fond of suffering; is it not so?"

Later on, when meeting any of the Sisters who happened to be ill or infirm, she would kiss the hem of her habit behind her back with the greatest veneration, looking upon her as the favored spouse of Jesus Christ.

One of the nuns, admiring the fervor with which this holy novice prayed with arms extended in the shape of a cross, asked her if the position did not cause her great fatigue.

"Yes," she answered with perfect simplicity, "it is rather painful, but don't say anything about it; they might stop me from doing it, and I am so glad to be able to do something for poor sinners. The first time I saw our Sisters praying with arms extended, I was so enchanted; it was the greatest happiness to me." And then when the Sister begged of her at least not to lift her arms so high in order to tire herself less, "Oh, no," she said, at the same time thanking her affectionately, "I cannot possibly do that." Once during her last illness, some one having asked her what she thought of suffering, she said, "Nothing is more agreeable in the sight of Our Lord; but how small is the number of those who love to suffer!" The same person, having been left with her during Vespers to take care of her, heard her addressing Our Lord in these words:

"My God, is there any other way by which I can get to Heaven, except by the Cross?" And then, having recollected herself more deeply, she went on: "No, no, it is by the Cross that Thou didst enter into glory, and it is by the Cross that Thou willest that we should arrive there. O my Jesus!" she continued, "with how many thorns hast Thou not strewn the pathway of those who wish to follow Thee?" In saying this she made signs as of a person who was feeling about and picking up something with much labor and difficulty; then sighing deeply, she continued, "But, my God, Thou goest too quick; Thou goest too quick, I cannot follow Thee; if I try to get on, the thorns pierce my feet and I can no longer walk. If I look at Thee, they enter my eyes and blind me." Then, after a moment or two's reflection, she said these words, "Everything passes away on this earth, everything passes away;" meaning, no doubt, that the time of trial is short, and the troubles of life, represented by the thorns which we find strewn on our pathway, should not discourage us nor make us slacken our footsteps on the road which Jesus has given us the example of treading, and to which He calls us.

The continual voluntary mortifications which she imposed upon herself are easily explained by her love of suffering. But it was not only in the practice of exterior mortification that she delighted; she found even greater satisfaction in what is also a thousand times more pleasing and acceptable in the sight of God, who looks above all to the sacrifice of will and heart, namely, in the practice of interior mortification.

A letter of hers, which has been preserved, dating from about the time of her clothing, shows some of the difficulties which she had to contend with, and also gives proof of the happy spirit in which she met them all.

"I was delighted to hear from you the other day. We have just finished Vespers, and my Mistress of Novices has given me permission to answer your letter. You have never thought, I hope, that I have forgotten you because you have not heard from me. But you know how little time a Religious can have for writing letters, and more especially a Poor Clare. I continually pray for you to the Sacred Heart of our dear Lord, that He may make known His Will to you, and that you may have grace and courage to follow it. Oh, N——, I am indeed happy; the Blessed Sacrament is exposed here night and day; we have Benediction every day, two Masses every day, and at night-time we rise to sing His praises. I will tell you a little of our life. We fast the entire year except on Sundays, and on that day we have two meals. Dinner is at twelve, and before and after dinner we say together the *Miserere*. We sleep in our habit; the bed is as hard as death, but I sleep very well notwithstanding. There are no lay-sisters here, we do all the work ourselves. The Mother Abbess herself goes nearly every afternoon to the kitchen to help clean the dishes with us. I go to the kitchen every day, and help to do the work; yesterday I cleaned the buttery, greasy dishes with my hands! It was torture at first, and I thought I should have been sick, but you know *for the love of God*, how powerful that is, and how easy all things become when it is for Him that we work. I sweep the stairs, also, every day. If you come here you will have to do all that sort of thing, and God will give you grace *to do it all with joy and happiness*.

"Every day we say the faults we have committed in the noviceship. The happiness here really surpasses all I ever thought of or expected I could find, and you know there is no true happiness without trials and without the Cross. Jesus is never without His Cross. Oh, do you not envy my beloved Teresa, gone so soon to her home? It was indeed a very great shock and suffering to me when I first heard of her death, but now I can only say, when I think of it, *Alleluia, Alleluia!* though I must add, I feel dreadfully inclined to envy her bright death. I feel she is always with me now, and I trust she prays that I may join her soon amongst the band of virgins who follow the Lamb. I thought of dear Maymie when I heard of her death. Roger told me she had felt it deeply. Best of loves to her and to all, and tell her I shall pray much for her. ... Ten thousand thanks for all your prayers for me. Let us unite together in spirit before the tabernacle in beseeching our Beloved Lord to have mercy on poor sinners. Farewell, dearest N——, ever pray for me; let us love the Lord Our God with our whole hearts while there is yet time—'A night cometh when no man can work.'

"Nearly our whole life is spent before the Blessed Sacrament. If you ever think of coming here, I advise you to take care of your health, as the Religious like postulants who are strong, for it requires a strong constitution to follow the Rule of our Seraphic Mother St. Clare. Pray hard that it may be the Holy Will of God that I may have sufficient health to take the habit, for I am afraid it is becoming an obstacle. Adieu."

CHAPTER VIII.

ON Sister Mary Clare's first arrival at the convent she had immense difficulty in getting accustomed to the food. Her natural repugnance to it was extreme, so much so as to cause frequent vomitings; but nothing abated her courage. Her greatest penance was to see herself better fed than the rest of the Community; she continually entreated that she might be served like the rest, giving as a reason that she would end by getting accustomed to it. Finally, she was allowed her own way. Notwithstanding this great repugnance, however, she would never choose those dishes which were most to her taste; on the contrary, it was always those she disliked most to which she gave the preference. If sometimes she sent away her plate, conquered by this feeling of nausea, she would instantly reproach herself for her faint-heartedness, and, sending for it back, would try hard to get a little down. Moreover, as if all this did not suffice to satiate her desire for mortification, she used to mix earth with what she ate, and put cinders into her soup and the rest of her food, begging at the same time her sister novice who used to see her doing it, "for the love of God" to say nothing about it. The Sister was so faithful to the confidence reposed in her that it was only after Clare's death that she spoke of it. She has also told us that Sister Mary Clare used to exchange with her little pieces of fresh bread, whenever she could, for stale pieces. On one occasion she ingenuously managed to secure and eat a piece of bread which she had carefully kept for some days till it was mildewed. When she was given something in particular which she rather liked, she used to say it was indulging her sensuality, and unless she was told to take it out of obedience she would refuse to touch it. One thing which at first cost her much to overcome, was to wash plates and dishes after dinner in the kitchen; it caused her the greatest nausea, and it was only by lifting up her eyes to God to ask Him to give her strength to conquer herself that she managed to get the better of her nature. "This practice is a great pleasure to me," she used to say, "because it may be made very meritorious for the conversion of sinners." Thus on Sundays, when her Mistress used to keep her at her side, she used to say to her, laughingly, " Yes, my Mother, it is all very well for you to say to me, 'Come, come,' but you know very well I want to go to the kitchen."

It was whilst suffering from these difficulties that she writes the following letter to her sister Gladys:

"I was so delighted to hear all about you from Madame de Nanteuil. I wrote yesterday to ——, enclosing a letter I had just received from Mary Bellasis, giving me an account of dear Teresa's happy death. I begged him to send it on to you. I hope you still continue to pray constantly for me to the Sacred Heart of our dear Lord. There are so many trials and difficulties in the religious life, that if He does not support me with His grace, I feel I shall never be able to remain here. The last few days the food disgusts me more than ever. I am cowardly enough (alas!) to wish to hide myself, very often, when the bell rings for dinner! One requires courage, but I hope always, and there is nothing one may not expect from the Sacred Heart of Jesus. It is enough to know that *His* power is unlimited, and He will never abandon me. From what you say about yourself I am sure Our Lord loves you very much. He gives you indeed a piece of the true Cross in those agonizing headaches you speak of. I am still very happy here, more so than ever, but you know the devil never leaves one in peace. I have much better spirits here than I ever had whilst I was in the world. I never felt really happy there, but here the very air breathes of the Blessed Sacrament. Once more don't forget to pray for me. Ask of our Blessed Lord that the day may come when I may be like a wax taper, silently consumed before Him in the Sacrament of His love."

When she was allowed the favor of wearing sandals, she always managed to leave them anywhere but on her feet; and when her attention was drawn to it she answered, "Oh, I forget them as often as I can." This was only in order to suffer the more; for summer and winter alike her feet were always icily cold, and in order to induce her to warm them, it was necessary to give her strict injunctions to do so; and even then she found means of mortifying herself afresh. When she lay down to rest, she managed so as to lie always in one position, declining positively to make herself more comfortable, and she was thus able to find an occasion of practising penance. She was greatly distressed at not being allowed to take her week in the kitchen in turn with the other novices and young Religious lately professed; and when it was represented to her that she was not strong enough to lift the heavy pans, she used to say, "but I am as strong as a giant." In the last days of her illness a Religious who was with her wished to give her a little cushion in order to raise her head. She refused it with a gentle smile; and when later on she consented to take it, it was because the Sister persuaded her to accept it with the intention of administering to Our Lord, suffering in her person, as in the same way St. Gertrude was persuaded to use some slight alleviation with the like intention.

Inheriting as she did, in all its integrity, the spirit of her blessed Father, St. Francis, who used to talk of "his Lady Poverty," she was, like him, fascinated by the beauty and charm of this virtue, and it would be hard to say to what sublime height she carried this spirit of detachment and self-abnegation.

Utterly dead to herself and to all created things, her heart was prepared to receive in abundance all those gifts and treasures promised to the "poor in spirit." Yes, it was whilst despising and trampling under foot all the vain and passing goods of this life that her soul entered into possession of infinite and eternal riches. God Himself became her sole good, her only portion and inheritance; finding in her a heart which was empty and void of all things, He took His delight in it, and made it the place of His repose. As our holy novice had never clung to any earthly tie, nothing ever troubled the calm serenity of her soul. In life, as in death, she enjoyed up to the very last a perfect calm and unalterable peace, precious fruits of her absolute detachment from creatures and her love of God.

"It is in vain," she said, shortly before her death, "that I search for motives which would inspire me with fear for the judgment of God; do what I can, I am never able to succeed in alarming myself; confidence in God always seems prominent in all my thoughts, and absorbs all others."

How, indeed, could fear have any hold over a heart which was so animated with generosity! Had she not given up all for God? Was it not for His sake that she had separated herself from her family, though she loved it so tenderly? Nevertheless these sacrifices which the world reckons so high were simply nothing in her sight; she reckoned all things "but as dung" that she might "gain Christ." *

Thus with what ardor did she embrace the practice of perfect poverty. Her sole desire had always been to become one day a "Poor Clare," because the most absolute poverty is observed in this holy Order, no one belonging to it possessing anything whatsoever, and the Religious living entirely on alms.

Shortly after her arrival, speaking to a young Sister about St. Francis of Assisi, she said, "The spirit of that great servant of God is the spirit of poverty. Taking example of him, I desire that holy Poverty, which he calls his mistress and queen, should also be my treasure and all my good." "I see you are too fond of our Father St. Francis," the Religious answered, "and are

* Philip. iii. 8.

too much animated by his spirit not to be sure of becoming his child."

"I would give anything to be one," she said. "My mother always told me I should become a Poor Clare; it was for that reason she gave me the name of Clare in baptism; hence my great devotion to that saint." A Religious asked her one day if, when she was living in the world, she expected to find such poverty as existed in the Order of Poor Clares. "No," she replied, "I did not think you would be quite so poor; but I am delighted to find it so, I am so fond of being poor; I am passionately devoted to poverty."

To give another instance. One day she manifested a desire to one of the Religious to write to her sister Teresa (afterwards a Sister of Charity), to beg of her to buy some pictures for her to distribute in the Community, when the Religious suggested to her that she had better ask her Sister to send her a little crucifix to put on the *prie-dieu* of her cell, in place of the cardboard one she had found there.

" Oh, no," she answered quickly, "I certainly shall not ask her that! I am so fond of being poor, I infinitely prefer that little cross to the finest crucifix in the world, because it is more in accordance with holy Poverty."

When she washed her feet (she would never consent to having any assistance in so doing) she used to take a piece of brick instead of using soap; and when she was given some common soap, she used to say, "I don't want that; pray give me my dear red soap, I prefer it to any other."

"I should think so," said the Sister to whom this was addressed, " because it is more according to holy Poverty, is not that the reason?" "This soap is not dear, and lasts longer; that is the reason why I like it."

Love of Poverty made her love the poor. "I was so pleased," she said, "when I came across poor people in England, I was always longing to be poor, too, and I should have been so glad to change dress and position with them; now that I am poor I am so happy."

When Sister Mary Clare arrived at Amiens, the Religious were much astonished on opening her trunks to find that she had hardly any linen, and the little she had was so coarse and common that many servants would have been better provided.

No one liked to ask her the reason; but, later on, of her own accord she acquainted the Mistress with it.

"When I was coming here," she said, "somebody told me that my linen was too fine and good for a Poor Clare, and that I should never be allowed to wear it; so I changed it with that of one of our servants. I also had the dress I wore when I came here made expressly for me, besides taking my maid's bonnet instead of my own, in order to be dressed more plainly. Papa, when he saw me in this get-up, began to laugh and tease me about it, but I did not mind a bit; on the contrary, I felt much happier in servant's clothes than I did in those I generally wore." It was with the same longing to be absolutely poor that she continually asked her Mistress of Novices to be allowed to give away the few little things she still possessed.

But the latter always answered that it was best to

wait till her profession, and that everything she had would then be given to the poor. This postponement did not suit her wishes at all; and on returning to the noviceship, after the ceremony of her clothing, she wished to cut up into little bits the embroidered pocket handkerchiefs which had been given her on that occasion. "I shall never use it again," she said; "I have shaken off all the vanities of this world." But her Mistress would not allow it, so she had to resign herself. Once when she happened to come across an old sandal, which was worn out and fit for nothing, she took it up and kissed it, as much from humility as from love of holy Poverty. A very short time after she had been allowed to walk barefoot, one of her Sisters in religion, seeing the great satisfaction with which she did so, said, "How pleased you seem to be with yourself! You look quite radiant!"

"Oh, yes," she cried, "when I was in London and I used to meet poor people in the street going barefoot, I used to think of the Poor Clares, and it used to make me quite envious, I was so jealous of them!"

"That is all very well at present, in the heat of summer," continued the Sister, "but when it is cold it is quite another thing. Nature will then assert herself. Now own, does she not already sometimes make herself heard a little?"

"Yes," answered she, "but I don't give her an opportunity of speaking long;" and then, with a vigorous thrust of her arm, "I say to her, '*Silence.*'" The determined voice with which she pronounced these words showed the great empire she already possessed over herself, and proved how little she yielded to nature in small things, as in great.

At the time when she was first attacked by the disease which carried her off so rapidly, being very susceptible to cold, some plain but warm woollen clothing was bought for her; this she only wore through obedience, and not without some distress, saying how much too fine it was, that no one else wore anything like it, and that she was no longer a poor Clare.

It was the same with regard to a blanket which was also bought for her about the same time; but again obedience triumphed over her love of poverty and of holy mortification.

Humility, according to the doctrine held by the saints, is only the courage with which we apply truths to ourselves with all their rigorous consequences. What then is truth as applied to man? It is that of ourselves we are nothing, since our being and faculties come from God, who at any moment can withdraw them. A slight disorder of the brain can cause the greatest intellect to lose his genius, the wisest man his knowledge and science, even to reason itself. Our virtue may succumb to the very first temptation, the slightest accident may destroy beauty; and this is because we possess nothing good of ourselves, since sin alone belongs to us by nature, and is our own: everything else comes to us from God, and must return to Him. . . . Finally, it is because we are of ourselves incapable of any good, even of a thought or a word useful to salvation, as St. Paul teaches; thus each one of us may say of himself, The evil I commit is my very own; but the good I do is neither absolutely mine, nor is it absolutely and purely good.

Sister Mary Clare had not only meditated upon these incontrovertible truths, but had long loved and practised them, and from them she drew the following definite conclusions:

Firstly, I ought not to esteem myself; on the contrary, I should have the lowest opinion of myself, reserving all honor and glory for God alone, who is the sole source of all good.

Secondly, I should not seek esteem and praise, they belong to God alone; to desire them for myself would be to desire that injustice and falsehood should be committed.

Thirdly, it is a duty for me to love a hidden life, humiliation, and contempt, because those are the conditions due to nothingness and sin, conditions to which Jesus Christ first submitted Himself, and to which we, following His example, should also submit ourselves.

It was upon these principles, which were strongly imprinted on the mind of our holy novice, that she regulated her interior life and her outward conduct. Actions with her responded perfectly with words. It was in these words that one of her Sisters formulated the judgment which all the Community had pronounced upon this chosen soul.

It was not enough for Sister Mary Clare to despise herself profoundly, she also wished to see herself the object of universal contempt. Learned in the schools of true wisdom, she recognized the vanity and nothingness of all the frivolous advantages which the world prizes so highly, and she generously renounced them in order to attach herself to God alone, desiring only His love in return.

We are fortunately able to give the following touching details regarding her profound humility.

On her first arrival she had been given in charge of a Sister, whose duty it was to help her to arrange her cell, and to dress herself, as well as to give her all necessary assistance. Sister Mary Clare soon discovered that an exception was being made in her favor; accordingly she would not suffer anything to be done for her, saying pleasantly that Our Lord did not come into the world to be waited upon, but to wait on others. She also cheerfully undertook all those little practices of humility which comprise the special duties of a novice, such as sweeping the staircases, cleaning and supplying with water the little fountain used as a lavatory; this latter she pretended was her special office, and she would not cede the right of attending to it to any one. She would not suffer any one to kiss her feet, as it is the custom to do on certain occasions among the Poor Clares; and one day one of the younger Religious having, whilst helping her to bed, found an opportunity of doing so out of reverence, she instantly rose, and kneeling down, exclaimed: "What have you done, Sister! I am going to pray to God to forgive you!" She had long implored of her Mistress of Novices to give her the penance of prostrating at the refectory door after dinner, as she had seen it practised by several of the nuns. How happy she was on that day when the Mother at last acceded to her wishes; with what pleasure she placed herself at the door of the refectory and saw all the Community pass over her! Her joy was such that after grace was over, meeting several of the nuns who had not been in the refectory at the

time her penance was performed, she instantly betook herself to the nearest doorway, so that she might induce them also to pass over her.

But what was even more worthy of admiration was the fervor of spirit with which she accomplished this act of penance. With her, the heart had an infinitely greater share than the body in these practices, and what might be for some a simple formality became with this upright soul the expression of an undoubted truth. Athirst as she was for self-humiliation, it was with much repugnance that she caused the smallest to others. Thus did she see any other Religious practising the penance of which we have just spoken, she instantly had recourse to various manœuvres to spare them a humiliation which she herself sought with the greatest ardor.

Not only meek, but also, like her Divine Master, "humble of heart," she asked of a young Sister, who was with her most frequently, to reprove her for her faults every time she should see her commit one, assuring her, if she did so, of her utmost gratitude.

"I will do it with the greatest pleasure," answered the other, " on condition you do me the same service."

"How should I be able to do that?" answered Sister Mary Clare; "I never can see other people's faults. I am such a sinner, I never can see any but my own!"

Some time before her clothing, when there was to be a deliberation on the subject of her admission, she said to one of the Sisters, "I do hope my health will not be the cause of my rejection." "Your rejection!" said the Sister, " we love you a great deal too much ever to be able to make up our minds to send you away."

"Oh, how good you are," said the postulant, "to be so fond of an abomination like me!"

Very shortly afterwards she happened to say without reflection, to a Religious who asked her how she felt, "My health is the only difficulty in the way of my admission, is it not?" But hardly had she uttered these words when the blood rushed to her face, and she quickly corrected herself. "What have I said?" she continued; "I am too great a sinner—I might even call myself a devil, I have sinned so much!"

Once, as she asked one of the nuns to pray for her, "Are you not our sister?" the Religious answered, "and as such could we possibly forget to pray for you?"

"What! do you look upon me as your sister?" she said instantly; "indeed, I do not deserve it; I am a wretched creature, a great sinner."

Some of the Community asked her the day after her clothing if she was happy; also, if her underclothing caused her much discomfort.

"I am perfectly happy," she answered; "this serge pricks me a little, but I am very fond of it."

"And your grand cord?" continued the other, "you don't say anything about that."

"Oh, that is also very dear to me," she said; and in pronouncing these words she put it to her lips and kissed it affectionately.

"Yet is it very hard and coarse, your cord," said the other, "it does not resemble in the least the beautiful girdles you used to wear in the world." "Oh, I did not care a straw for those girdles I used to wear in the world; I certainly never kissed them out of love!" Then another nun, who knew what pleasure she was giving her by saying something a little humiliating, appearing to doubt the truth of her words, said, "I should have liked very much to have been present to see if you are really speaking the truth."

When she said this, an expression of joy lit up the countenance of the dear novice as she sweetly answered the person who doubted her, "Oh, thanks, thanks, dear Sister, for your just opinion of me!"

A short time before her death she desired the Mistress of Novices to burn all her letters; and she herself tore up every prayer she had composed, so that they might be known to none but God.

What are we to say of Sister Mary Clare's obedience? Humility and obedience may be said to be sister virtues, and it is as difficult to imagine humility without obedience as it is to conceive obedience without humility. All men who know and despise themselves submit themselves to the yoke of obedience. Is not obedience also the shortest and quickest road to God? Is anything more pleasing to Him than the sacrifice of our own will? Are there any means more secure of protecting us from illusion, than to do the will of those who hold the place of God in our regard? Sister Mary Clare cherished the virtue of obedience and found her happiness in practising it; still, she had to work in order to acquire this virtue in all its perfection, not only because in her own family she had always had her own way, but also because, being very fervent, she had a great desire, notwithstanding her feeble health, to embrace all sorts of penances and mortifications, and it was therefore necessary to restrain her.

In her early beginning she had difficulty in submitting herself, and some of the same prohibitions had to be repeated twice ; but from the time of her clothing the whole Community had cause to admire the complete change which was operated in her in this respect. From that time she had no longer any will of her own; it was sufficient that a desire was expressed to her for her to submit at once joyfully, and with simplicity ; for with her, obedience was joyous, prompt, and firm. Her greatest fear was to be wanting in the smallest degree in the practise of this virtue. But if obedience oftentimes imposed a sacrifice on her fervor, she knew how to make double profit of it by adding to the merit of the good action she had been desirous of performing the still greater one of obedience, by which she immolated her will itself to the will of God. Anxious as she was to adorn all her actions with the precious merit of obedience, if sometimes such a thing happened to her as to forget to ask leave to perform any action, she at once repaired her omission by redoubled submission and humility. As for charity, as it would be impossible for any one to have a great love of God without also loving his brother, we may judge what was Sister Mary Clare's love for her neighbor. It was a real happiness for her to do anything to oblige one of her Sisters ; indulgent, she judged favorably of all the world ; devoted, she was ever ready to render any one a service.

But it was, above all, for the good of her neighbor

ENTRANCE FROM THE COURTYARD OF ST. CLARE'S

that she was so anxious to sacrifice herself. Sinners before everything were the objects of her solicitude; with what fervor she prayed for them, with what sorrow she followed their wanderings and their follies! The thought, above all, of the infinite misery that awaits them for all eternity was always urging her to offer herself up as a victim to obtain their conversion. After sinners, her greatest love was reserved for the poor and the afflicted, remembering the words of her Master, " Whatsoever you do for the least of these little ones for My sake you do for Me." Every day, after dinner was over, she could be seen at the door of the enclosure carrying two dishes, one of which contained the soup and the other vegetables, which, according to the habit of the Community, were distributed among the poor who presented themselves there to receive alms. Always the first to arrive in the kitchen, for fear that she should be robbed of this welcome task, she acquitted herself of it with equal joy and alacrity.

Conscious that recollection is one of the conditions of an interior life, and that it is in silence that God makes Himself heard in the soul, Sister Mary Clare had a most special attraction to the practise of this virtue. She spoke very little, as a rule, but when she did so it was always to the point; being convinced that it is impossible to spread one's self much abroad without losing the Presence of God, and without committing a multitude of little faults, which tease, if they do not stain, the conscience, she spoke little to man, though much to God.

She was heard once to express herself thus with regard to silence: "I must seek God, I must find God; but where shall I find Him?" After entering into herself for a few moments, she added: "It is in silence; God speaks to the soul in silence, and it is in silence that the soul enjoys God. Our Lord does not wish that we should diffuse ourselves abroad, because, if we do, speak as He may to our hearts, we do not hear Him." She also said: "There are two things which are extremely necessary to the soul which seeks perfection; one is to fly the conversation of creatures, the other to seek that of God."

Thus with what love she cherished silence, how faithful she was to observe it! She carried this fidelity during the retreat before her clothing to such lengths as not to wish to answer except by signs, unless addressed by her Superior.

To die and to die soon, that was her great desire, her daily longing. She testified it continually, and on all occasions. "When shall I go to my only Home," she used to say, "to possess my God? It is so tiresome being upon earth!" When she heard the news of her sister Teresa's (in religion Sister Magdalen) death, she was quite unhappy at her dying before herself, and was full of envy at her happiness. Her Mistress told her then that it was quite fair that her sister should be beforehand with her, since she was her elder, and ripe for Heaven, and that accordingly the same grace would be given her as soon as she had reached that degree of perfection to which she was called, and that she must therefore work at detaching herself more and more from her own will, and uniting herself more closely to Our Lord and Saviour.

These words consoled her greatly, and she showed much good-will in trying to put them into practice in order to gain the much-desired reward.

On one occasion she was speaking to one of the Religious of her desire to die. "Death will come some day," answered the Sister, "but perhaps that is not what would be most pleasing to Our Lord, and if you love Him truly, you will only desire what is most for His honor and glory."

"I should not ask to die," said the novice, "if I knew for certain that I should give more glory to God by living. But no one could persuade St. Philip Neri, whose zeal for the conversion of sinners was so great, to ask God to prolong his life in order that he might continue his labors. Only St. Martin is known to have said to Our Lord that he was ready to live in order to work for His glory and the salvation of souls. If you could see into my heart you would understand how much more I should glorify God by dying than by living longer."

This desire for death, however, was not with her the fruit of a self-love which only longs to escape further labors and sufferings. If, like St. Paul, she longed "to be dissolved," it was only because her body was an obstacle to her perfect union with her heavenly Spouse.

This same longing desire showed itself in other ways. She used always to like to shut the windows of the attics, and, whilst doing so, would remain there long in contemplation of the heavens; and when it was remarked to her that it was contrary to the rule of enclosure to look out of the windows, because they were in front of houses from which the Religious could be seen, she was much astonished to hear any mention of houses in front, for the simple reason that she had never even so much as seen them!

Often, when she was in bed at night, she used to ask that the curtains of her bed might not be entirely closed, so that she might see her dear sky.

"When I first get to Heaven," she said one day towards the end of her last illness, "I shall be out of my mind with joy. With what ecstasy I shall throw myself into the arms of Our Blessed Lady! The angels, seeing me do it, will be quite astounded, and they will ask each other, 'What does she mean by it?' I shall answer them, 'Ah! if you had only lived in that land of exile as I have, if you had only suffered in a mortal body as I have done, you would not be astonished to see me transported, as I am at this moment, with joy and happiness because this body, which separated me from my Beloved, has at last fallen from me like an old worn-out garment, and is now no longer any obstacle to my union with Him.'"

CHAPTER IX.

SEVERAL days, meanwhile, had passed away after the 15th of October, the happy day of our dear sister's espousals with her heavenly Bridegroom, and we had even begun to entertain some hopes (said the Religious who gave us these details) that with care her health might be able to accustom itself to our austere life, when God, who appeared up till then to have supported her physically for the time, seemed to hearken to the longing desires of His spouse in calling her without further delay to her eternal nuptials.

Her health was seriously affected, first of all, by a cold, which was accompanied by fever. The doctor, who was at once called in, had no hesitation in pronouncing it to be a pulmonary attack, from which there was little or no chance of her recovery.

What joy this news brought to the dear Sister Mary Clare of the Infant Jesus! At last her prayers were heard—she was to die! Her joy was so great on hearing it that her only fear was lest her satisfaction should have so favorable an effect on her health as to bring her back to life again. It was not enough for her to know that she was going to die; the three or four months, assigned as the limit of her existence by the doctor, already seemed much too long for her to live.

" Death will have nothing to say to me," she used to

say; "pray, then, to our good Lord that He may take me quickly to Himself."

Sufferings she counted as nothing, and, far from dreading them, she received them joyfully; but the great, the terrible sacrifice for her was to behold the moment put off when she was to be set free—the term of her exile.

"I was quite sure," she used to say to the Religious at about this time, "when I came to ask to be admitted here, that I had not long to live. It was the motive that made me so anxious to persuade my father to let me enter the Community; my vocation was to die here."

Although Sister Mary Clare was thus willing to make this last sacrifice that God asked of her—that of her life—it is not to be supposed that her father could hear, unmoved, of the alarming state of his daughter's health. The hopes which he had built upon the general improvement of her health for the first six months of her joining the Community at Amiens were suddenly dashed to the ground, and, in writing to the Mother Abbess, he expresses his great anxiety in the following terms:

November 8th, 18—

"MY DEAR MADAM:—The accounts which I receive of my daughter's health are so distressing that I cannot refrain from writing to you on the subject. Willing, as I am, she should embrace any life, however austere or painful, to which God may call her, I cannot consent to her doing anything which would be distinctly the cause of her death, for this I do not believe to be the will of God. She is bound to preserve her life, however anxious to sacrifice it, and I, too, as her father, am bound to protect it against her indiscreet and youthful fervor. I know how painful a blow it would be for her to be sent home from her convent; she would prefer dying; but it is not a question of *choice* but of *duty*. I therefore, madam, appeal to you whose experience and whose special graces in your position enable you to form a sounder judgment and opinion than I can at this distance; I appeal to you whether my beloved daughter Clare ought to continue any longer in her present course of life. Perhaps the accounts which I receive are not very accurate or authentic. Perhaps, as she wishes to believe, she is surmounting her difficulties and trials. If so, may God be praised. But if, on the other hand, her constitution be sinking, and her life ebbing under her austerities, I feel that it is my imperative duty to save her life, and snatch her, however reluctant, from the grave. You will write, I know, with entire truth and sincerity, to,

"Madam, with most profound respect,
"Your most humble and obedient servant,
"JOHN VAUGHAN."

The Mother Abbess's letter has not been preserved, but we have no difficulty in guessing its contents. The doctor's decision had already anticipated it. For Sister Mary Clare's illness there was no cure. She was attacked by the rapid decline which had already carried off one beloved sister, Teresa, in the spring. The austerities, of which her father speaks, were not accountable for the terrible hereditary disease which she bore in her veins, and which she already knew a violent cold or exposure of any sort was extremely likely to rouse to active mischief. She writes thus to her father on the subject: "You have heard from our Mother Abbess that the doctor has pronounced my recovery impossible, and that I may at any time receive Extreme Unction. I cannot resist writing to tell you with what immense happiness this glorious news has filled me. My only grief is to think of you, my darling papa, and of all the loved ones at home, who cannot yet share my happiness.... I am in *subdued agonies* * for Heaven. I think it must be our darling Teresa who has obtained this grace so soon for me. Do you remember how she used to mimic my intense horror *in case the Poor Clares live long?* O papa, I cannot tell you how inexpressibly happy I am! In a few days I shall take the vows. All my desires are being accomplished, and I can only thank our beloved Lord for all His infinite mercies. When you see Herbert, do ask him to offer up Holy Mass for me. I will pray so immensely for you when I am in Heaven, and will try and console you, my own darling papa."

About a fortnight later she writes again: "I cannot tell you how delighted I was to receive your letter this morning. Your letters always fill me with joy, though I cannot help the tears starting to my eyes. Our Reverend Mother begs me to say that she is waiting until the doctor has seen me again, before she writes to give you an account of my health. He is coming on Saturday. At present he is absent from Amiens. I feel myself much about the same, though rather weaker than

* A favorite expression of Clare's, which she was in the habit of using on all occasions.

last week. What a happiness to see you again, my *more than beloved* papa, as you speak of coming, if my illness becomes serious; but you could only see me at the grille; as for entering the infirmary, nothing less than a permission of the Pope could effect it! Our Lord came to me again in Holy Communion this morning in the infirmary, which was unspeakable happiness. Though I cannot kiss your beloved face, and tell you so a thousand times, there is not one of your children who loves you with such intensity as your devoted child, Sister Marie Claire de l'Enfant Jésus.

"The nuns pray so much for you here! One old nun came to me this morning, and said she heard that you travel a great deal, therefore she constantly prays that no accident may happen to you."

The state of weakness in which Sister Mary Clare found herself increasing daily, and the doctor who attended the Community having given his opinion that she might at any time be carried off by a sudden turn of her malady, it was thought prudent to administer the last Sacraments to her. Also the permission on which all her hopes were centred was granted for her supreme joy and consolation, namely, that of being allowed to make her Solemn Profession.

"It is the one happiness I long for," she used continually to repeat; and on one of the Sisters asking her whether she thought they had done the Will of God in receiving her in the state of health she was in, she answered, "Oh, yes! you have certainly done the Holy Will of God in receiving me; all my hopes and desires were to die a Poor Clare, and Our Lord has heard them."

It is in the following terms that Clare announces her approaching death to her uncle, Father Edmund Vaughan.

December 6th, 18—

"I would certainly have written to you before this, and have thanked you for your two letters, but you do not know that during the great Advent of St. Martin, which begins on All Saints and lasts until Christmas, we are not allowed to write letters, though we may receive them. I am astonished that I have enough patience to explain all this to you when I have such *glorious* news to tell you, namely, that I may hope in a very short time—in a few days, perhaps—to see my celestial Spouse in Heaven, and to gaze forever on that Face, the beauty of which no words can tell. I am writing to you from my bed, ill in the infirmary. The doctor came to see me last Saturday, and said my recovery was an impossibility, and that I might at any time receive Extreme Unction. He says that not only my chest, but everything in my body is attacked. My illness began by a cough two days after my clothing; and about a week or two after I took up my abode in the infirmary, and since then have not left it. ... Our beloved Lord comes to me in Holy Communion here in bed, which is inexpressible happiness. I am going to make my vows and receive Extreme Unction in a few days—perhaps even this afternoon. Is not all this unspeakable happiness for me, dearest Father Edmund? The longing, burning desire of my heart to see my beloved Spouse *so soon* to be realized! I have a great deal to tell you, but feel so weak that I cannot write much more. How I will pray for your poor sinners when I have arrived at our eternal Home! Excuse this dreadful writing. Pray a great deal for me, particularly when you hear of my death. I have not been able to write to dear Kenelm to tell him of my happiness. You and papa are the only two I have written to. Do not forget *prayers.* Do ask Father Coffin to say Mass for me after my death."

A few days before Clare's profession, Colonel Vaughan, who had been informed at once of the critical state of his daughter's health, wishing to see her once more, came to Amiens.

It was at the grille of the choir that Sister Mary Clare—by special dispensation, she being at the time only a novice—was taken in an arm-chair to this last interview. The first words addressed to her by her father recall those once spoken by the last of St. Bernard's brothers, when his brethren took leave of him before plunging into the solitudes of Clairvaux : "How happy you are," he said, "my daughter ! You are taking leave of earth in order to go to heaven."

Earthly things had no share in their conversation; he only spoke to her of God. If he could not quite conquer his emotion at seeing his daughter in such an alarming state of health, it was at least consoling to his Christian heart to contemplate the peace and happiness which she enjoyed even in the midst of the privations that the rule of life which she had embraced imposed upon her. As for her, no greater sorrow could have been caused her than to have proposed to her to quit her holy retreat in order to return to the paternal roof. Her one wish was to remain in the monastery to the last.

Thus terminated this last interview, the results of which had been much dreaded by the Community for Clare's health, in consequence of the emotion it was expected her father's presence would cause her. But, dead as she was to all earthly things, she saw only God, and had no thoughts for any one but Him. And yet she loved her father very tenderly. One day she had been heard to say, " My God, Thou knowest how much I love my father, Thou knowest all I suffer at not being able to see him once more, to embrace him; but, O my God! Thou knowest I love Thee more—yes, infinitely more !" Earthly affections had no longer any power over her heart! Jesus alone reigned there as king; alone He filled it to its utmost capacity, as alone He occupied every thought and wish in her mind and soul. Her body was indeed still on earth, but already her soul was in Heaven.

When her eldest brother, the Reverend Herbert Vaughan, then an Oblate of St. Charles, came to see her on his way to Rome, no outward sign betrayed her feelings; not that she was indifferent to the pleasure of his visit, but because grace alone worked in her—she loved only God, and, for His sake, those who were united to her by ties of blood.

Thus when, the following morning, this dearly-loved brother gave her Holy Communion, she did not so much as cast one look upon him. Father Vaughan was so struck with this instance of her profound detachment, that he could not help remarking upon it to the other Sisters outside the enclosure when Mass was over.

The conversation she had with her brother at the grille

ran on exclusively heavenly things; it was their last farewell before separating on the great journey to eternity.

After leaving Amiens, Father Vaughan wrote the following account of her to Gladys:

"I have seen Clare; she was brought into the church carried on a chair; very thin, much changed in face, like Joe, as he was four years ago. Her voice was very faint, but in other respects she was her old self, but very weak. She spoke about you and about Teresa. Her eyes were all the time fixed upon the Blessed Sacrament. I did not stay long, as I feared to tire her. Next morning I went into the monastery and gave her Holy Communion in her cell.

"She may yet live for several days. I should not be surprised even if she lingered on a month. Her great mortification now is not to pray, or ask for death, but to be resigned to God's will without asking to die.

"She is immensely happy; nothing could exceed her joy; but she is purified, chastened, and perfected, and therefore improved, and ready for admission into the bosom of the Lord Our God.

"Let us pray to God that we, too, may become purified and perfected here in this world."

Sister Mary Clare's great desire was that the Feast of the Immaculate Conception should be chosen for her Profession, and also that she should receive the last Sacraments upon it.

Her wish in this choice of a day was to put herself more particularly under the protection of Our Lady, and to obtain from the intercession of this all-powerful

Mother the grace from her Divine Son of dying on her Feast.

She therefore begged all the Religious to unite with her in a Novena to the Immaculate Conception to obtain this grace, submitting, however, the circumstances and time of her death entirely to the will and good pleasure of God.

The day of the Feast having arrived, she received the last Sacraments from the hand of the venerable Superior of the house, assisted by the chaplain, with sentiments of the liveliest devotion. She answered all the prayers with the greatest fervor and clearness of mind, and her fervor was redoubled, if possible, in pronouncing her solemn vows. All who were present were struck by the holy eagerness with which she took the book presented to her by the Rev. Mother Abbess; no one could forget the happy smile which lit up her face, and the thrilling tones with which she pronounced the formula of her vows.

From that day to the day of her holy and beautiful death God alone occupied all her thoughts; prayer succeeded prayer, one spiritual lecture followed another; still, she never showed the smallest symptom of weariness or fatigue; her patience never gave way for one instant during the whole course of her illness, which lasted nearly three months. Her infirmarian, as well as her other Sisters in religion, could not sufficiently admire how in the midst of her sufferings, acute as they were, not only she never uttered a complaint, but not even a shade was seen to rest on her countenance. Always calm and contented under all circumstances, whatever

INTERIOR OF CELL WHERE CLARE PRONOUNCED HER VOWS, AND DIED.

noise was made around her, whether any one spoke, or left the door open or shut it, conscious as she was of the inconvenience, it mattered not. Her infirmarian had to be most careful to provide for all her wants; she never manifested any desire, and was always satisfied with everything.

If any comfort or alleviation was offered her she almost always sought to avoid accepting it; and if she availed herself of it, it was only through obedience. A few moments before breathing her last sigh, she glanced towards the window, and said: "It is very cold, is it not?" A Sister, perceiving that her hands were cold as ice, presented her instantly with a hot-water tin. "Perhaps," she said, refusing it, "it would be better to suffer this slight discomfort"; but the Mother Abbess, having told her to use it, she submitted at once, thus uniting to the last the utmost obedience with mortification.

Doubtless it would cause astonishment that Sister Mary Clare, who had been so carefully brought up, and whose constitution was by nature delicate, should carry mortification to such lengths, if one did not know what the love of Jesus Christ can work in a soul when it takes entire possession of it. As, according to Our Lord's own words, no one can give a greater proof of his love than "to give his life for his friend," the soul which is once inflamed with this divine ardor no longer lives: her life is a continual death, and her only desire is to make a victim of her body in order to be immolated night and day at the altar of divine Love.

Sister Mary Clare always showed the greatest gratitude for all, even to the smallest, services which were rendered her. One night she happened to be more than usually suffering, and speaking to the Infirmarian, who was sleeping close beside her, she cried out, "Quick, quick, Sister, I am going to be sick." Hardly had she uttered the words than she regretted them deeply, and the next day she said to the Infirmarian, "What could you have thought of me last night? I was indeed very troublesome, and showed very little spirit of penance." The Religious at first could not imagine to what she alluded, and only begged her to calm herself, and make every possible use of her services.

The Mother Abbess, seeing her one day a prey to the acutest suffering, said: "Perhaps you would not have asked to die, if you had known all the pain you would have to go through first." "Oh, yes, dear Reverend Mother," she answered, "that fear would never have prevented me from asking the grace to die!" Though her sufferings were at times almost greater than she could bear, she would have been quite willing to see them increase, not precisely to hasten the moment of her deliverance, but so as to be able to answer in the words of the Apostles, when Our Saviour addressed Himself to them and asked them if they could drink the chalice with Him, "Yes, O Lord, if only Thou givest us the strength."

Thus it was that she begged one of the Religious who watched by her bedside to pray that she might have a long and painful agony. The moment, however, was not far removed, and it was by the renunciation of the most ardent desire of her heart—to die speedily—that she prepared for it, thus preferring in that, as in all things, to abandon herself to the good pleasure of her Lord and Saviour. Two or three weeks before her death she takes farewell, in the following letter, of the dear sister who was next to her in age, the changed and trembling handwriting showing how much the effort cost her. It was her last letter.

"I am going to write you a long letter, to beg you not to grieve too much when you hear of my death. Only think, when I am in Heaven we shall always be able to talk to each other, whereas here we can never see each other or talk easily together. Our Lord loves you very tenderly, very specially, dearest Mary, for He leads you to Himself along the way of sorrows; and I am sure He and His sweet Mother will console you, and will teach you to bear generously and heroically for their sakes the heavy trials He sends you. Our Lord Himself says by the mouth of His prophet, 'As one whom his mother comforteth, so will I comfort you, and you will be comforted in Jerusalem.' Courage, then, darling, courage! The greater your suffering, the greater will be your crown, and then you will have the special love of Jesus and Mary. No one knows how *deeply* I feel for you. You will be the first one in my thoughts when I reach my eternal Home. I will beg Our Lord not to leave you long on earth. Offer up your sorrows in union with the sorrows of the suffering Heart of Jesus for my soul after my death. Do get oceans of prayers for me. I am so *intensely* happy at the thought that I am so soon going to die! How immensely loving of Our Lord to take me so soon, is it not? I am sure your only joy in the world will be to adore and watch before the Blessed Sacrament. It is in that treasury of grace you will find all your strength and consolation, as I have found from my own experience. Do you remember before I came here how often I used to say to you: '*Take all that shall be brought upon thee, and in thy sorrow endure, and in thy humiliation keep patience*'? Now I wish I could say something to make you laugh, and to send away the tears from that dear pale face. Do you remember. ... Do not forget that this letter is intended for you. I am writing it by scraps every day, as I feel extremely weak—too weak to write a long letter at once.

"*Thursday.* Since I began this letter I have seen another doctor, who says I may yet live another month. Kiss the two darling little ones, and tell them never to forget Clare, but to pray for her every day, and then she will pray for them in their home in the skies! Ask Smith when she is going to be a Catholic. Give dear old White my love, and ask her to pray that I may make a happy death, and that I may not only be saved, but that my soul may not pass through the flames of Purgatory. Prayer is all-powerful, and may obtain even that. How you must *long* to be a nun! I like the Order you have chosen, or rather I should say the Order God has chosen for you. I think it is a good thing for the two little ones that you stay with them still for some little time, especially for———. Does your governess take you to visit the Blessed Sacrament every day? If so, it must be a great comfort to you. It is He alone who can console you, and it is He alone who knows how to sympathize with every human grief; and your grief will be turned almost into joy when you think that when your heart is almost breaking with sorrow it is then that you are a subject of envy to the very angels and saints, because of your likeness to the Man of Sorrows."

On the evening of the Sunday in the Octave of the Epiphany a violent crisis in her malady took place, and it was thought by all that she was very near her end. She remained some time unconscious, and it was only by means of *eau de cologne* and other stimulants that she could be brought round. All the Community was assembled in prayer round her bedside; when she saw herself thus surrounded, she exclaimed, "How sweet it is to die like this!" She answered aloud the invocations in the Litany of Our Lady, and on the Abbess saying to her, "Courage, my child, courage! death is not far off, your crown will quickly follow." "It is all very well to say, 'Courage, Clare, courage!'" she answered, "when as yet I can only see Heaven through a tiny little hole"; in saying these words she explained her meaning by holding up her hand half-closed, so that only a little scrap of daylight could be seen through it.

"In fine," she continued, "I am still a long way off"; and she was right, as the alarm, serious though it was, passed off.

Regular in her habits and obedient to the last, she would only take her nourishment at the same hours as those when the Community took their meals. A quarter of an orange, some fruit at the beginning of her illness, after that a little lemonade, and some spoonfuls of soup (meagre) was all the food she took; it was impossible for her to keep anything else down.

One day she was given a little piece of chocolate when she could not take any other form of nourishment.

"Oh!" she exclaimed, "I could not eat all that; it would make me live too long, and I am longing so to go"; and she left half of it.

At last the eve of the 20th of January arrived, the Feast of the Holy Name of Jesus, and the day when our dear Sister Mary Clare of the Infant Jesus was to join the virgins "who follow the Lamb whithersoever He goes," to sing with them the immortal canticle with which they alone will make the heavenly vault resound.

Having had the happiness of communicating that morning, she received a visit early from the Mother Abbess, who asked her what Our Lord had said to her in coming to visit her, and whether He had told her that He would come to fetch her that day.

"Our Lord made me feel," she said, "that He took such pleasure in my sufferings that I did not dare to ask Him to take me away with Him."

She had frequent and terrible vomitings all day long, and towards night her weakness became very great.

About seven o'clock the Mother Abbess came to her bedside with a great part of the Community, and from that time she never left the dying Sister till she breathed her last. All prayed fervently for her intention. Sister Mary Clare preserved full consciousness till the last. She herself begged to be allowed to renew her vows, and did so with the greatest fervor. About nine o'clock she turned her head to those of the Community who were obliged to leave in order to say Matins, and to go to take their hour of adoration, and said, with a gentle smile, "Adieu, my dear Sisters, adieu." Then she added, "Pray"; and then again, with a most touching expression to the Mother Abbess and the Sister nearest to her, "Pray for me, I am dying." And when it was represented to her that she was exhausting herself by trying to speak, "Never mind," she said, "pray, pray."

She herself, in her holy impatience to possess her Beloved, ceased not to send Him faithful precursors in the ardent transports of her loving heart.

Her crucifix never left her lips; she kissed it incessantly with inexpressible love and affection. About half-past nine the Mother Abbess asked her how soon she thought she would die. "In about two hours," she said, "Our Lord will come and fetch me."

It was about half-past twelve, whilst the choir were singing the third Nocturn of the glorious martyrs SS. Fabian and Sebastian, that her beautiful soul took flight on the wings of divine love for the regions of the heavenly Jerusalem, there to drink deeply of the torrent of delights with which God rewards His chosen ones. A few moments before breathing her last, her countenance suddenly assumed a celestial expression, she took an attitude of profound respect, and made signs to those who were with her to follow her example, saying some words at the same time which they did not understand, and of which they had not the presence of mind to ask her an explanation. No doubt, faithful to His promise, Our Lord had come to welcome His beloved Spouse, or had deputed, as He has sometimes done with regard to other holy souls, a heavenly ambassador to meet her and take her into His presence.

After Sister Mary Clare's death an angelic smile still appeared to hover round her lips; her forehead, pure as alabaster, presented a symbol of innocence and purity to all who saw her; whilst a voice seemed to say to those Mothers and Sisters, who, kneeling round her bed, shed a last tear and said a last prayer: "Weep not for her; she is not dead, she sleepeth."

The following prayer, composed by Sister Mary Clare, was found under the monstrance where the Blessed Sacrament is exposed night and day before the grille.

"O Jesus, my sweet and only Love, hearken to the ardent prayer of a most unworthy sinner, who is also Your child, Your betrothed, and Your spouse. I beseech You by Your Heart, burning with love for sinners, and in honor of the Sacrament of Your Love, to grant that my chest may be *soon* attacked, and that I may die and go to You, my dear, dear Master, my Beloved. I am too unworthy for You to listen to me, miserable sinner that I am. But I confide in Your enormous love and in Your mercy. I know, O Jesus! that if I trust in You I shall not be confounded. O Jesus, increase my faith! My only sweetest Love, help me, and be merciful to Your devoted and unworthy spouse, Sister Clare of the Infant Jesus, Victim of the Blessed Sacrament."

Bishop Brownlow has just published the Memoirs of Mother Mary Rose Columba Adams, O. P., First Prioress of St. Dominic's Convent, and Foundress of the Perpetual Adoration at North Adelaide, in which he quotes a letter of hers, written to a friend Dec. 31, 1889, in which she says:

" The life of Clare Vaughan made a great and a very good impression. I am so glad we shall have a copy of our own. It was the ardor of her charity, not austerities, that caused the bodily frame to fail, the keen spirit cutting through its sheath of flesh; she *must* immolate herself, it was a kind of necessity with her. Death was truly an entrance into life. I can quite believe she would rejoice really, I might say naturally, when she knew she would not long be detained here. It is a life that carries conviction with it, so true was the intensity of her love. I often offer her love to our dear Lord, and tell Him that I wish I had her faith and love, though I know I am not worthy of such gifts as were hers."— *From Memoir of Mother Mary Rose Columba Adams, O. P., by the Right Reverend W. R. Brownlow, Bishop of Clifton.*

www.ingramcontent.com/pod-product-compliance
Lightning Source LLC
Chambersburg PA
CBHW031456160426
43195CB00010BB/1001